POP CULTURE HERETIC

MORALITY THROUGH A SCREEN

FICTIONAL INFLUENCE
BOOK 1

KRISTIN MCTIERNAN

Shirkley Press

CONTENTS

Cover designed by Juan Padron of JCOVERS.COM

Printed in the United States of America

❀ Formatted with Vellum

AUTHOR'S INTRODUCTION

As lightning to the children eased
With explanation kind
The truth must dazzle gradually
Or every man be blind

Emily Dickinson knew better than most the power of story. It's the one constant among humanity: Truth hurts. Best to soften it with a riveting tale.

I started writing about pop culture in 2014, just as the culture wars were heating up—when millennials started taking over newsrooms and Hollywood writer's rooms alike. Back when we all agreed to the polite fiction that stories don't shape us, that we're too smart to be influenced by something as silly as a superhero movie or a horror film.

Right around the time a lot of writers dove hard into politics, I focused on stories. Fiction, it turned out, was a better teacher than any politician. Better than any teacher, camp counselor, or clergy too. And sometimes (not all the time) even better than my parents.

Movies didn't care about protecting my feelings or preserving my innocence. They didn't worry about whether I was "ready" for certain truths. They showed me what people actually do when they think no one is watching, what humans become when the pressure gets high enough, and how evil presents itself in the real world.

My parents tried to prepare me for life. My teachers meant well. The clergy had good intentions. But none of them were willing to tell me the things I actually needed to know: that nice people can be monsters, that victims aren't always innocent, that sometimes violence is the only moral choice, and that most people will choose comfortable lies over uncomfortable truths every single time.

Fiction told me all of this and more. It did what the adults around me wouldn't—it treated me like I could handle reality. Sometimes it was wrong, to be honest.

I've never really been okay after seeing *Seven*, for instance.

The essays in this collection represent my ongoing attempt to decode the lessons in our entertainment. They're not film criticism or academic analysis. They're field reports from someone who learned to use fiction as a survival guide, a moral compass, and a bullshit detector all rolled into one.

You won't find any particular political ideology or religious framework here. I've written as a liberal feminist, a conservative Christian, and everything in between. Truth doesn't care about your tribal affiliations and it always manages to shine through, no matter how ideologically captured writers become.

If you're looking for someone to validate your existing beliefs, you've bought the wrong book. These essays will piss off progressives and traditionalists in equal measure.

They'll challenge atheists and believers. I know this because my Substack has a comments section. And boy, is that a lively place.

That's the point.

Fiction doesn't coddle you. If it's done right, it shows you what you need to see, whether you like it or not. These essays attempt to do the same thing.

This is the first compilation, a curated selection of the weekly essays I publish on my Substack at fictionalinfluence.com. It's the kind of book you can read on the toilet instead of doom scrolling on Twitter. Read one entry, put it down, and then pick it up again later.

Or you can binge it in an afternoon when you're supposed to be paying attention to that all-hands Teams meeting. It's okay, I don't judge.

Enjoy the ride.

Kristin

PART ONE
FAITH IN STORIES

CHAPTER 1
DO YOU LOVE GOD, OR JUST THE STORY?

PROMETHEUS, the 2012 prequel to Alien, was a massive failure of film editing. So much was abandoned on the cutting room floor, it left the audience scratching their head about what the hell was going on in this trainwreck of a movie.

Shame on everyone who let it happen.

It wasn't until the movie novelization, director's cut, multiple clarifying interviews, and some amazing think pieces that the genius of the film really came to light.

We had to wait on that clarifying content to realize that the way the script presented humans' reaction to meeting "God" was nothing short of brilliant, which is why the most famous quote from the film is an anguished Dr. Elizabeth Shaw screaming, "We were wrong! We were so wrong!"

In short, *Prometheus* is a story about humans going to quite literally meet their maker. Our maker, as it turns out, isn't so much interested in meeting us, as he is intent on wiping us from the face of the universe. When the crew of the Prometheus ship arrives on the planet on which Shaw believes our Gods reside, they find something far closer to hell than heaven…

There in the derelict ship, they finally meet an Engineer–the last of his kind, perhaps–and when they wake the sleeping giant, he's not very happy to see us… Weyland commands David to ask the Engineer for the secret to eternal life, because "Gods should live forever," and in the face of such hubris, the Engineer rips David's head off, and bashes Weyland to death with it. - Dom Nero, *Esquire*

Prometheus isn't the first work of science fiction to grapple with the question: What would it look like for humans to meet their creator? The consensus seems to be that some measure of mourning, if not despair, will come of it, even if our creator isn't some violent creature who actually hates us.

The level of benevolence of the God/Creator figure doesn't seem to be what causes the despair, but rather the pain of a human's ego, lashing out at being wrong.

The folly of man's ego is a predictable conflict in science fiction, particularly in those stories dealing with God, humanity's creation, and its destruction. We spend our lives seeking out God in one way or another, and these stories allow us to explore what would happen if we presume to go looking for Him before He is ready to be revealed.

Most importantly, the stories invite us to examine how we would react in the face of such a discovery and what it says about who we are.

Childhood's End by Arthur C. Clarke is a famous example, one that slaps humans with a double-whammy of ego-bruising. "Yes, your religions were based on us and you didn't get it quite right. Also, your time in the universe is up. Collectively. Sorry."

A more recent example is _Broken Gods_, by B.R. Keid. It's the final book in the military scifi trilogy, one that looks at a far-flung future where humanity's "god" is a female alien mysteriously called The Twelfth.

The Twelfth of what? How did she save humanity from the destruction of earth? And why? In _Broken Gods_, the main character, Sev, finds out the truth about a religion he never even believed in. But it still leaves him unmoored.

SINNERS IN THE HANDS OF AN ANGRY GOD

Having faith means projecting certainty in things about which you have not observed with your own eyes. It means being convinced by the accounts of others, by your own feelings, and by the preponderance of existing facts as you perceive them. So what does it mean when this faith you have upheld turns out to be wrong?

Can the human ego endure the truth of something so large?

Imagine a Reformed Baptist being presented with Divine proof that the Roman Catholic Church IS the one true church and he has been in error this whole time.

His soul is safe; God is forgiving of error. But will that be enough for him? Will he rejoice and be glad at having the truth revealed to him?

Or will he mourn, even rage, at the loss of the identity he has created for himself?

Prometheus showed us the folly of humans who think to become gods themselves, allowing us to see the absolute silliness of such an idea. You, fragile, finite creature... a god? Please.

Broken Gods took us down a different path, one I won't spoil. But it took a hard look at the human ego and exactly what would happen if humans were blessed with a chance to look God full in the face... only to find it wasn't quite what we imagined.

Almost. Partly. But not completely.

It lets us take a good look at our hearts, our egos, and our intellect.

Is it God we follow? Is it God we love?

Or is it just the stories?

Best to take stock of that sooner rather than later.

CHAPTER 2

ATHEISM WILL GET YOU KILLED

"ARE YOU RELIGIOUS AT ALL?" *the old woman asks our protagonist, taking a long drag on her cigarette.*

"I try to keep an open mind," our protagonist responds.

The old woman smiles lightly, a clear look of victory flashing over her features.

- The Skeleton Key (2005)

In our modern secular times, authors often neglect the religion or lack thereof of their characters. This is a mistake, one that can hamstring your storytelling.

High fantasy and (of course) Christian fiction authors tend to incorporate religion and use it to fine effect. Other genres... not so much.

But faith dictates far more than what you do with Sundays and leaving it out entirely can leave your characters hollow at best, and behaving unrealistically at worst.

ATHEIST WRITERS MAKING ATHEISM A CHARACTER FLAW

Three of my favorite examples of faith being used as a major plot point were actually written by atheists. So this isn't about proselytizing for a specific religion or world-view. It's understanding the limitations of an existing belief system. And how it can get you killed.

I already mentioned *The Skeleton Key*, which used the MC's lack of conviction against her. She believed in nothing, so the bad guys were able to successfully impose a belief system on her. This resulted in her losing not her life, but her body.

It wouldn't have happened if she had a strong existing belief system. Even if she had been an ardent atheist, she would have been okay. But she wasn't. She was malleable, open-minded. And as a result, she lost all that she was.

The Orville—which started off as a Star Trek spoof but ended up as a space-faring masterpiece in its own right—did something similar.

ALL of the characters in *The Orville* are atheists. In the show, religion is treated as a relic of the past, a silly superstition. This lack of belief in an immortal soul is exactly why Captain Mercer (and the rest of the crew) welcomed a Kaylon onto their ship. Kaylons are sentient androids. They are notoriously xenophobic and avoid "biologicals." But then, all of a sudden, one decides to work on Captain Mercer's ship on a supposedly diplomatic posting.

The robots are sentient but they don't have souls. They do not believe that humans or other living beings are special or unique. They do not believe in an afterlife. They do not fear death.

But they are counted as intelligent life by the enlightened crew of the Orville and they are shocked—*shocked!*—when the Kaylons come to kill them all. Just because they can.

They might be self-aware, but they're not human. If the

crew, even one of them, believed in the concept of a soul, the majority of Season 2 and 3 wouldn't have happened.

Finally, the paranormal thriller, <u>The Autopsy of Jane Doe</u>, makes the MC's logic, reason, and atheism a tragic fatal flaw.

Our MCs are an aging coroner and his grown son, who he hopes will take over his business. And they are called to determine the cause of death for a young woman. No one knows who she is and no one can tell how she died. The body looks untouched.

With every cut, the two men are baffled by what they find. How can her lungs be burned while the outside of her body is undamaged? And what is this old piece of parchment that has been shoved down her throat?

I knew what it was. I knew almost immediately. But our MCs didn't. They never stated outright they were atheists. But it was obvious. They are clearly not Christians and didn't believe that witches are real, or ever were.

By the time they understand what they're dealing with, it's far too late.

If they had been believers, the plot couldn't have happened.

THE CHARACTER'S FAITH IS ALWAYS IMPORTANT

Don't think because you're writing a cop thriller, this doesn't apply to you.

Your hard-boiled detective has seen so much and sometimes feels like he's lived too long. He doesn't believe in God or the afterlife, not one bit.

Fair enough. But the way you write this guy cannot be the same way you write his partner, who has also seen too much, but is a faithful Catholic.

One believes that there will be an accounting of actions and final judgment after death. One does not. Having these two characters behave the same way and base their decisions on the same moral framework is lazy writing.

This isn't just a question of your character's morals. Those are ALWAYS relative. Even among Christians, we argue over morality. The question of your character's faith should be used to inform the **behavior** you write for them.

This could be a major plot point, or it could just be a personality tic. Either way, it adds depth and richness to your characters and, in some cases, can give you a fantastic plot twist for the story.

Regardless of genre, always consider what your character believes about the nature of this life and the next.

It makes for a better story and a deeper impact on the viewer.

There's a reason shows like the X-Files run as long as they do.

CHAPTER 3
YOUR CULTURE IS BUILT ON FICTION

IN THE 80S AND 90S, there was a popular trope in movies, TV, and church-related improv groups that played out as follows:

- Nice Kid is being bullied by Mean Kid
- Nice Kid asks adult for help with harassment and physical assault
- Adult tells Nice Kid that Mean Kid is abused at home / is an orphan / saved puppies from a fire. Adult advises Nice Kid to make friends with Mean Kid.
- Nice Kid apologizes to Mean Kid (for being so punchable, I guess) and makes overtures of friendship.
- Mean Kid accepts. "I guess we're not so different after all."

What absolute psychopath decided this was the message that a generation of kids needed to hear? And why did the thousands of people across the media and cultural landscape go along with it?

It's a good question to ask, especially now with the overt brainwashing people in the entertainment industry have been perpetrating on children and adolescents. Who exactly is informing your child's morality?

IT'S NOT JUST "YOUTHFUL IGNORANCE."

If you're a parent of an older child, you've probably had the moment when your kid says something completely contrary to the way you raised them.

"Where did you hear that?" you ask, baffled at this ridiculous, uninformed opinion that they seem so certain of.

"Everyone knows that. You're just ignorant!" Your previously loving child might say.

Who is *everyone* in this scenario? Probably their friend group… all of whom consume the same media—a movie or a show. Or TikTok.

Unless you're very careful, media has more time to communicate directly with your child than you do. Works of message-laden fiction have the power to mold your child's mind in ways you wouldn't want. And even though you're grown now, and probably intelligent, these messages still influence you too.

The effects of these messages are not short-term.

THE SAME STORY TOLD REPEATEDLY BECOMES TRUTH

In another article, I told you about how I underwent surgical sterilization in my 20s. (You can read the complete account in Evie Magazine). At the time, I was not married or even dating. There was no chance I would fall pregnant. So why was I so set on that permanent preventative measure?

Because the 1990s (when I was an adolescent) was a rare moment when the religious right and the left-leaning entertainment industry agreed on a social issue: **Having a baby will ruin your life**.

Churches and religious organizations, in an attempt to dissuade teens and unmarried young people from having sex, emphasized how a woman's life would be ruined were she to fall pregnant.

- The man who impregnated you would leave you. Or abuse you. Or both.
- No other man would want you because... ew
- Your friends would also leave you, as you're no fun anymore with that baby
- All your dreams will crumble to ash because the baby will take all your time.

These sentiments were bolstered by schools, both in sex ed classes and in the essays and educational videos they assigned. Again, targeted at reducing or eradicating unwed teen pregnancy.

But the real kicker was the entertainment and media industry. They piled on with their rotation of Monday Night Movies of the Week (now playing on Lifetime Movie Network), which emphasized that men would either abandon you outright or use your baby as leverage to continue abusing you.

Feature films like *15 and Pregnant* emphasized the mistake of teen pregnancy, but there were many more that showed adult, married women being destroyed by having a baby as well. Glossy mags targeted at girls (Teen, Seven-teen) extolled the virtues of single, unwed, and childless women and how happy they were, while telling nightmare stories of abusive boyfriends and the horrors of being abandoned after having a baby.

The message was clear and universal. Having a baby will ruin your life.

INTENTIONAL MESSAGING

The film and media industries aren't falling into these ubiquitous messages accidentally. It's quite intentional, make no mistake. And as humans, we are all susceptible to that messaging... even if you're a religious person.

Even if you're in church leadership.

Though I am still religious, I have a great deal of loathing for 90s purity culture precisely because it took its cues from the anti-child, anti-family media landscape at the time, trying to be hip and cool as it burdened a genera-tion with lies.

Christianity has always been firm that sex is something only to be shared within marriage. Anything outside of marriage is sin. It's not a new rule or one confined to the 90s, when I was a teen. What was unique to that time (I think), was the emphasis on pregnancy as the PROOF you had sinned, rather than the avoidance of sin itself.

Pregnancy was a scare tactic because if you got preg-nant (and you definitely would, according to them), you wouldn't be able to hide what you'd done. Pregnancy is bad, not just because of the shame, but because of the baby that would result.

The baby itself was painted as punishment for the sin

of premarital sex. "You don't want to be like those sad girls in the movies, do you?"

Those lessons don't fade away after you grow up and get married.

I've said many times that fiction makes us better people. It personalizes morality and philosophy in ways that spur emotional growth.

But it can also lie to us, to make us feel like everything is hopeless and rotten, and we may as well give up. Which is why choosing what you consume is of utmost importance.

That bestselling book might not be good for your kid to read. And that blockbuster movie not be good for you to watch.

Never think you're above the brainwashing, because none of us are.

CHAPTER 4
DAREDEVIL AND UNMASKING FAITH

THE QUESTION of what constitutes "real Christianity" has raged in media for the last few decades, often splitting along political lines. In seeking clarification, most look to their favorite priest or pastor for guidance. But if you've grown disillusioned with Church leadership, there's another, less conventional source of clarity regarding Christian goodness. Netflix's Daredevil. Specifically, season 3.

The sadly final season begins with a strong and unapologetic nod to the original comic: its focus on Matt's faith, or in this case, his loss of it. In the last episode of The Defenders, a building fell directly on top of Matt Murdock, AKA Daredevil, as well as Elektra, the love of his life whose soul had been stolen by The Hand.

This should have been fatal, to say the least. It wasn't. By the grace of God (and yes, I mean literally), he was carried away from the wreckage in a drainpipe, found by a cab driver, and taken to St. Agnes' Church... the orphanage where he grew up.

Until this crushing defeat, Matt lived his life with the certainty he was walking the path God laid out for him. He believed God selected him to be the Devil of Hell's Kitchen, the protector of the weak. Now, Matt is not so sure.

HITTING ROCK BOTTOM

Matt's ability to "see" is gone, as his entire sinus system has been severely damaged by the explosion. He doesn't know why or how he survived and, as his recovery continues at a too-slow pace, he realizes he wishes he didn't. After all, if he can't be who he was made to be, then he doesn't want to be at all.

For Matt, the idea that God did not choose him to be a protector is shattering. It is made all the worse when he discovers Father Lantom and Sister Maggie, his mentors and guides in his faith, have been lying to him since he was a child.

We watch how his inner changes are reflected in his outward behavior. This was another brave and true point the writers made.

If you change on the inside (your beliefs, your outlook, etc.), you WILL change on the outside.

The behavior of a person who believes in one God, the Father the Almighty, will always be different from a person who believes we are merely hairless primates. It must.

GOD AND YOUR IDENTITY

This is something we don't often admit because, as Westerners, generally we value our secular society. But it is true and it's why I say that many people who consider them-selves to be believers... really aren't. Let me explain that before you get mad.

Often when you meet a self-identifying Christian, there is no difference between them and your atheist or agnostic friend. If you were to ask one of these believers how their life would change if they WERE an atheist, they have no answer for you.

Would your friends change? The media you consume? The clothes you wear? No. Nothing would change. Because you live like an atheist. Noted atheist Bill Maher got it exactly right when he said the majority of Christians are not followers of Christ, but merely fans.

But Matt DID believe. And the loss of his belief changed him. He estranged himself from his friends, from his mentors, from his calling. He abandoned his commit-ment to preserving life, succumbing to the idea that murdering Kingpin is what is right. Except he knows it's not right; it's just what he thinks will make him feel better.

Swallowed up by nihilism and self-pity, he becomes a different man. It is only when he comes face to face with a true devil, his mirror image, that he can see what he has become.

Though Matt finds peace with himself and his place in the world by the end of the season, it's not stated clearly if his faith has actually returned. But I think it has. Because of how he behaved:

He forgave a good man and a good woman who lied to him because they genuinely thought it was right.

He saved his city without committing murder

He accepted the love of his friends, giving of himself to those who needed it most.

Matt Murdock shows us that real Christian faith is not just the "still, small voice," it is what we do and how we treat one another.

"By their fruits, you will know them." (Matthew 7:16)

PART TWO
CORRUPTION AND FALSE PROPHETS

CHAPTER 5
MIDNIGHT MASS: THE ALLURE OF GROUPTHINK

THERE ARE few creative voices in the filmmaking world I trust these days. By trust, I mean if I see their name attached to a project, I go see it. I buy a ticket to movie theater or, if needed, subscribe to a particular streaming service.

Mike Flanagan was the reason I subscribed to Netflix after a long absence. *Midnight Mass* is one of several limited series helmed by Flanagan. It can reasonably be classified as a religious, supernatural thriller, similar to his other series, *The Haunting of Hill House* and *The Haunting of Bly Manor*.

Like those shows (which I also enjoyed), *Midnight Mass* is about so much more than a mysterious new priest in town or the reasons behind seeming miracles. It is about faith, the dangers of zealotry, and the need to examine ourselves at the deepest levels.

If you intend to watch it, I recommend you do so before reading the rest of this, because I spoil the whole thing.

Midnight Mass takes place on a small New England

island accessible only by a twice-daily ferry. After an oil spill that decimated the fishing industry in the area, the island has shrunk to a population of less than 200. It is run-down with an aging population. The few children on the island are just looking for a way out and the adults are worn down from decades of hard, physical work and financial woes. But they have their faith.

Nearly all the residents are Catholic, though only a few are devout enough to attend Mass every week. They've had the same priest for several decades.

But when the old man goes off to the Holy Land for a pilgrimage, another, younger priest comes back in his place. The Monsignor has taken ill, the younger priest says. And he, Father Paul, has been sent by the Archdiocese to stand in for him while he recovers.

Shortly after Father Paul arrives... the miracles begin.

- A teen girl confined to a wheelchair walks to receive the sacrament
- An elderly woman with dementia begins to recover memory and her physical ailments also improve
- Father Paul himself dies of what appears to be poisoning...only to come back to life

These signs and wonders are observed by the tiny island and word spreads: God is with us on Crocker Island. Come and be faithful.

And they do. The whole island (except the Muslim sheriff, the Atheist prodigal son, and a few skeptical others) go to Mass every week. Their faith is restored, as are their bodies.

And it never occurs to them. None. Of. Them. That

these signs and wonders might be coming from something other than God.

It is in this narrative backdrop that Mike Flanagan gives us a set of rules, or perhaps guidelines would be better to say, about how to live righteously. These rules are for everyone: The fervent Catholics crowding into Mass, the discouraged Atheist looking for redemption, and for everyone in between.

GROUPTHINK CAN KILL

There comes a point in the show where the mask is fully off Father Paul. He reveals completely that he is following his own will, his own desires, rather than God's. And he is using cherry-picked, out-of-context Bible passages to justify the horrendous things he has done and plans to do. At one point, he stands in front of a packed church giving a repulsive, blasphemous Good Friday homily, and I was overcome with supreme sadness.

The whole congregation, except one person, listened to that garbage... and nodded along. Because they had watched a young paralyzed girl walk. Because they no longer needed to wear their glasses or their back no longer ached. They saw the signs and wonders and they couldn't see anything else.

They attacked anyone who tried to point out "God doesn't work like this." They ignored their lifetime of sitting in Mass and listening to Jesus's words, his warnings, about false prophets. And they felt justified because the only people who rejected Father Paul were already outsiders, already misfits.

By the time anyone in the in-group realized how wrong they had been, it was far, far too late.

DO NOT PRESUME TO STAND IN GOD'S PLACE

Father Paul spends the majority of the show firmly in the wrong. Everything he does is so, so wrong. But he convinces himself that it is right. More than that, he convinces himself that God approves.

When he tells lies to the congregation about who he is, he asks God for forgiveness for the lies "he must tell in His service." When he kills a man, he says that his lack of guilt over it is proof that it is God's will. We watch both him and Beverly use scripture to justify the choices they have made instead of using it to guide them. And it is horrible to watch how assured he is.

In the end, he realizes what he's done. Too late. He put himself in God's place and justified it however he could because he was afraid. Of growing old and dying. Of missing out on a life he wanted but couldn't have. He was an old man looking back at his life and wishing it could have been different. There is an order to things. And he decided that it didn't apply to him. Too bad he wasn't alone in paying for that hubris.

ADDICTION (TO ANYTHING) CHANGES WHO YOU ARE

The show starts with one of our protagonists, Riley Flynn, being sentenced to jail time for accidentally killing a girl while he was driving drunk. It is the guilt of this and his subsequent loss of faith that gives Riley such a clear view of what is happening in his home town. His addiction was alcohol, but the show goes much further in its condemnation of addiction than a simple matter of drunk driving.

In the last episode, when we discover what the "sacrament" really is and what it does, we have to watch in horror as good, decent people are overcome with a hunger they can't control. At the end, when reason once again returns, a young boy numbly tells a man, "I think I killed my mom." The man can do nothing but nod and comfort the boy, standing by him as they grapple with their lack of control and the horror it has wrought.

POWER IS THE STRONGEST DRUG OF ALL

"You aren't a good person, Bev... God loves everyone else just as much as he loves you. Why does that bother you so much?"

The villain in this series is Beverly Keane (played by Samantha Sloyan). Not the supernatural menace in the shadows. It's Bev. This horrendous, power-mad woman was a "Karen" in the best of times, using scripture as a weapon to stand in judgment of everyone for everything. For what they wore, for how often they came to mass. For even daring to have a pet dog when she didn't decree him to deserve such a thing. We have all known a person like this.

They use some other authority to beat down those around them. In Bev's case, it was religion and her position as a church official. In other people's case, they invoke secular ideas like "common decency" or "public health." All with the idea that if you don't obey this person, then you are evil. And you deserve to be punished.

Giving someone power, even a little of it, is the truest test of character there is. And unfortunately, it seems the majority of people fail that test.

The final rule is only for Christians. But if you identify as one, listen up. And listen close.

THE PARADISE CHRIST PROMISED US COMES IN THE NEXT LIFE, NOT THIS ONE.

Anyone who tells you that if you are obedient enough, good enough, faithful enough, that you will be rewarded with riches and protection from tragedy... they are not of God. And they are selling you something.

Just a week before I watched *Midnight Mass*, I watched *The Way Down*, a docu-series on HBO MAX detailing Gwen Shamblin and her Remnant Fellowship Church in Tennessee. If you saw it too, you probably noticed many similarities between the fictional Bev and the real-life Gwen. How they held themselves above others, how they felt empowered to decree who was worthy and who wasn't.

Ostensibly, the Remnant Fellowship Church is in the Church of Christ denomination. This is not one of those non-denominational churches that seems to make up their own rules. They have a firm (and strict) theology. So why did the majority of the congregants sit back and allow this? Why did so few leave? And the ones who did leave... it was only after they were ostracized within the church.

We saw the same thing in Midnight Mass. Though a fictional story, it tells us a nasty truth. We are willing to believe anything, as long as it comes from someone "on our side."

Even though we have been explicitly told about "the prophet, which shall presume to speak a word in my name, which I have not commanded him to speak" (Deut. 18:20), still we fail to remember what we've been taught.

Just give us something we want, show us something "miraculous," and it seems we fall like the walls of Jericho.

The power of a good story is that it makes us think. It

helps us realize who we want to be. And who we were all along. So watch *Midnight Mass* and *The Way Down*. Watch the signs of deception, both real and fictional. And ask yourself, truly, if you would behave any differently. I so fervently hope that I would.

CHAPTER 6
HERETIC: THE VULNERABILITY OF LITTLE GIRLS

Bjørn: *Why are you doing this?*
   Patrick: *Because you let me.* —From *Speak No Evil* (2022)

THE GREATEST FILMS always leave themselves open to a number of interpretations, and the newly released horror movie, *Heretic*, is no different. Terrifying, thrilling, and oddly funny in spots, the ending leaves you wondering what it all meant, what you're supposed to do now, and if you're like me, will probably leave you wanting a second viewing.

Most of the YouTube commentariat has rendered the firm verdict that *Heretic* is a plain-faced attack on organized religion, a misogynist institution designed solely for men's benefit and women's detriment. The thriller is just the set dressing for the message, they say.

You might be surprised to hear me say this after reading some of my other work, but I disagree.

Heretic begins with two fresh-faced Mormon missionaries going door to door attempting to convert people to their church. Unlike many evangelical organizations whose missionaries are comprised of elder married couples (often with grown children), the Mormon church sends young adults—pairs of boys or girls—most of whom are naive, untested, and unused to the vulgarity of the secular world.

Sister Barnes and Sister Paxton (their first names are never given and these girls never address each other by their Christian names) arrive at the door of Mr. Reed (first name also never given), ready to answer all his questions about the Church of Jesus Christ of Latter Day Saints.

After coming into his home, only after being assured his wife is baking a pie in the next room, Mr. Reed offers them soft drinks and says, "I think it is GOOD to be religious."

We find out later in the movie that, yes, he most certainly does think it is good to be religious. For the girls anyway. For his prey.

The question is why.

We got a hint early in the movie alluding to what I think the message of the film is. Before Sisters Barnes and Paxton arrive at Mr. Reed's house, they see a trio of pretty girls filming a TikTok in the middle of a crosswalk.

Sister Paxton, the blonde, eagerly rushes up to them, ready to get her first documented baptism. The girls are eager to take a picture with Sister Paxton, but then rip off her skirt, exposing her Mormon "Magic" underwear. And they run off laughing.

It's just so funny, committing sexual battery in the open street. And filming it! And probably posting it to their followers.

I seethed in the theater, boiling over with the need to get in their (fictional) comments and make sure those little bitches were canceled so hard they got kicked out of college.

Because we all know why those girls felt so comfortable doing that to poor Sister Paxton. I doubt little miss TikTok would have dared try to rip any piece of clothing off a heavy-set trailer park girl.

They did it because they knew they'd get away with it. They knew the sweet Mormon girl wouldn't knock their teeth down their throat.

It was a display of power. Nothing more. And it was very in line with the overall theme of the movie.

FEEDING GIRLS INTO THE MEAT GRINDER

The innocence and ingrained accommodating nature of the Mormon missionaries plays a prominent role throughout the film. Some will point to the girls stepping inside Mr. Reed's house without actually seeing his wife, but I think this is the least stupid thing they did. In their place, even now in my decrepitude, I would have too.

At this point there were solid green flags. A friendly man in a nice house in a nice neighborhood, a living room with a homey decor that reeks of a woman's touch. It all looks legit. And Mr. Reed is so friendly, charming, and yes, handsome. There was nothing to put them off… except the normal human refusal to step inside a stranger's house.

I find it borderline hilarious that the LDS church criticized this film, saying: "Any narrative that **promotes violence** against women because of their faith or undermines the contributions of volunteers runs counter to the safety and wellbeing of our communities."*

---

* Kessler, Mori (2024, Nov 16). 'Heretic' film prompts LDS church

To accuse a movie of endangering their fresh-faced 19-21 year-old missionaries is quite a stretch.

YouTuber (and former Mormon Missionary) Alyssa Grenfell does a great job of breaking down why the LDS Church itself is the one placing these girls in harm's way. It is not only their age and the fact that the missionaries are sent into dangerous places at home and abroad; it's also the sheltered way in which they've been brought up.

Both actors in Heretic are former Mormons and their performances were perfect. Sister Paxton in particular had the sweet, encouraging way of showing interest when she spoke to Mr. Reed that most men would interpret as flirting.

I have known many Mormon girls in my life, especially in middle school, where Southern Baptists reigned supreme and Catholics were called Mary-worshippers to our faces. It made sense that we would be friends with the Mormon girls.

I went to services with them (obviously never the Temple). Their families gave me the whole spiel. I love my Mormon friends.

And I prayed and cried every day they were on their missions. I could tell they censored their letters about how it was going. (Gary, Indiana is where they were sent, if you were wondering).

Unlike the evangelicals, the Mormons send little girls who have likely never been kissed and are as innocent as can be into all manner of dangerous neighborhoods.

Of course the Mormons don't like the movie. It shines a

response from Utah officials regarding missionary safety. *St. George News.* https://www.stgeorgeutah.com/life/religion-life/heretic-film-prompts-lds-church-response-from-utah-officials-regarding-missionary-safety/article_bf5c6bae-a3b2-11ef-84d6-cf6a1f69c791.html light on the danger they put these girls in for NO reason. Muslims are growing faster than Mormons. They don't send young girls into foreign countries to strangers' doors.

Muslims ALSO don't lie to their girls and tell them that if they love God enough, then they will be safe. And neither do most evangelical missionaries. The married couples who go to Cambodia, Pakistan, or any other number of hostile places accept they may die for their ministry and have accepted that risk to spread the word of God.

These young girls have been told from birth that there is no risk, that they will be personally protected by Heavenly Father if their heart is true.

This is a vicious lie that can only be told if you hate young girls with your whole heart.

Did God find Polly Klaas deficient? I think not.

It's sickening to tell this to the most innocent among us and is tailor-made to make pliable, cooperative victims.

Thus brings us to why Mr. Reed selected his victims the way he did.

SUPPLANTING GOD INSTEAD OF SEEKING HIM

I don't think it's too much of a spoiler to say that Mr. Reed obviously spent many years studying religion. Not just Mormonism; from the looks of it, he studied ALL of them, going back as far as he could.

Impressive, I suppose, except when you consider WHY.

It was not to seek God, to understand His plan, and how Mr. Reed should fit into it. It was to decipher which of the religions best facilitated his own unearned authority and which one(s) ensured willing and pliable victims.

He wasn't wrong that Mormons were the best option on BOTH counts.

Mormonism isn't uniquely bad, not in general and not towards its women. But its beliefs are structured in a way that attract bad individuals. The belief in personal revelation is a huge problem, for one. Unquestioned male headship is another.

The insular nature of how Mormons are raised and that they remain child-like in their beliefs on human nature far longer than most others puts the final nail in the coffin.

The first moment Sisters Barnes and Paxton start to feel uneasy with Mr. Reed is when he asks them about polygamy, specifically if they actually believed Joseph Smith was given the green light to marry all those women he wanted to sleep with, or if he made it all up to justify his adultery.

The girls were uncomfortable with their church doctrine being questioned. But that's not actually what Reed was asking.

What he was really asking is "Do you believe in personal revelation?"

Because if the answer is yes, that makes his plan smooth sailing.

The danger of personal revelation was also seen in *Under the Banner of Heaven* (a non-fiction book turned semi-fictional mini-series). The show looked at a real crime committed by members of a highly respected Mormon family, one of whom asserted God spoke to him. And what did God say?

You guessed it: Have sex with your underage stepdaughters. It's cool, bro. I'm God.

Funny how God ALWAYS tells these "prophets" that

serving him means having sex with a bunch of young girls.

The problem with personal revelation is that you can't disprove it. You can only attack the "prophet" himself. And if the "prophet" is popular, you just might get yourself killed, which is what happened in the mini-series. And real life.

The already-atheist movie reviewers who gleefully assert that *Heretic* is an attack on religion, missed the message. They missed what the ending meant.

They missed that it wasn't a condemnation. It was a call to action.

Being strong in your faith means being learned in its history so you can spot straw men and other assorted nonsense. It also means standing up for your faith and yourself.

"Turn the other cheek" doesn't mean be everyone's personal bitch. And "Let he who has not sinned cast the first stone" does NOT mean just let everyone do whatever they want to you, your family, and your community.

Two things can be true at once.

1. God is real and religion is how we make sense of Him AND
2. Evil men exist and they use religion as an effective vector of controlling and silencing their victims

The film insists that you can be pure of heart, a true and faithful believer... while also stabbing a mother fucker in the neck when you need to.

CHAPTER 7
MAYBE GOD DOESN'T LOVE YOU

DIRECTOR KEVIN SMITH enraged the religious right (especially Catholics) with his 1999 movie, *Dogma*. Though Catholics were probably right to suspect Smith's motives (Hollywood atheist, of course), the central plot tenets and the fallen angels plan centered around taking Church law and the fact of Christianity seriously. It was religious humans who were mocked, not God Himself. (Yes, God was portrayed by Alanis Morrisette, but the script made clear God is NOT a woman. Or a man).

Undeterred, Smith went on to make another movie that heavily featured religion in 2011. Red State is an action horror movie that involves three teen boys who are kidnapped by a violent fundamentalist doomsday church (modeled off the Westboro Baptist Church—The God Hates Fags people). Lured by the promise of no-strings sex, the boys are held captive with the intent of being hate-crimed as part of the church services.

But things don't go as planned. For anyone.

The movie, as it appeared in theaters, started off strong,

but was largely forgettable. It ended oddly. Fell flat. Didn't seem to be saying anything. I was left flummoxed at my initial viewing.

But then I heard about the original ending. The one Kevin Smith scrapped, supposedly due to lack of funds.

Then it all made sense.

Originally, the movie would have ended with the Four Horsemen of the Apocalypse descending to Earth to unleash divine wrath upon both the cult *and* the government agents. Everything the cult predicted was correct, in other words.

For the record, I don't believe Smith when he says it was a only budget issue. I believe he chickened out, stamping out the mic-drop ending that would have sent shockwaves through his liberal fanbase. And through Bible colleges as well, I suspect. Sure, money was a factor. Smith is an indie filmmaker, after all. But he's also a wokie. He was happy to enrage Christians with *Dogma*.

But I don't think he had the spine to answer when someone inevitably asked him, "So are you saying the Westboro Baptist Church is right?"

It's a shame, really. If he had gone through with it, the film would have had the kind of impact and staying power that _Frailty_ did.

What does it mean when your least favorite parts of the Bible turn out to be TRUE?

THE FIVE POINTS TRINITY CHURCH

The movie starts us off from a purely secular point of view. We see the family members of the Five Points Trinity Church picketing the funeral of a recently murdered gay man and our nose wrinkles at the all-too clear memory of the WBC doing exactly the same thing (as well as to KIA Iraq war veterans). We hear a high school government teacher use the group in her lesson about the first amendment: "[Abin Cooper] holds our whole state up for ridicule. Even literal Nazis condemn him!"

As a Kansan, I felt that. The Five Points has a universally unpopular message. No one likes them or wants to hear what they have to say.

So what do they have to say? A full 20 minutes of the movie is devoted to a sermon by Abin Cooper, a recounting of his beliefs and grievances with his family members paying rapt attention, nodding, smiling, and praising Jesus at Cooper's words.

Our kidnapped teenage boys, on the other hand, are held in metal dog crates at the edge of the pews, hyperventilating as they beg to be let go.

Abin is unmoved. He continues his sermon (between playful, grandfatherly chiding with the small children in the sanctuary), recounting the tale of Noah. Specifically how it serves as a condemnation of modern preachers and their soft faith.

"God loves everybody? If God drowned the entire world, does that sound like He loves you?... It's a God that abhors the wicked and those who disobey... God don't love you. Unless you fear him! You better believe *I* fear God. My fear is born out of respect, sacrifice, adoration, and knowledge of the scripture."

He does not blink from scripture, doesn't recoil or mitigate or apply a modern lens. Nor does Smith (in the script) alter scripture or inject disinformation. Everything Abin Cooper says is in the Bible, explained properly and in context.

It's only when the pretty teenage girl is asked to take the small children out for their lessons that the service takes a turn from your average fire-and-brimstone congregation.

With the children safely out of the room, Cooper pulls a sheet off what we assumed was a crucifix. And it is.

Except there's an adult man tied to it, a gag in his mouth. Apparently, this is a gay man, one we didn't meet until now. "We're gonna deal with them as God taught us to deal with them."

Cooper specifies that the command against killing is actually a command against murder. But murder is something that can only be done to humans. "This is not a man. This is an insect. The commandments don't apply to him."

Then Cooper and the other men murder this gay man as he begs for his life, prompting the captive boy to scream: "I ain't gay!" in a futile plea for his life.

"You might be worse!" replies Cooper. "You came here to share a woman [another man's wife] with other men on the same day. You're already dead, Sinner."

So you see, God does indeed hate gays. But from Abin Cooper's reading of the scripture, He hates you too.

THE DILUTION OF THE CHURCH AND SCRIPTURE

The X-Files episode "Signs and Wonders" is one of my favorites due to it's (much lighter) condemnation of pastors who tell their congregants what they want to hear instead of what their faith actually teaches. Regardless of what type of Christian you are, you know what I'm talking about.

When God's angel says: "So, because you are lukewarm, and neither cold nor hot, I will spew you out of my mouth," (Revelation 3:16) that's exactly what he means.

And when Jesus said, "For narrow is the gate and difficult is the way, which leads to life, and few find it," (Matthew 7:13-14) He meant that too.

You wouldn't know it from listening to these rock star pastors wearing $900 shoes. Do these verses sound like they were written at the behest of someone who is interested in the self-help schlock that fills stadiums and calls itself *real* Christianity?

This is where there's a false divide between professing Christians (people who believe) and atheists/agnostics (people who don't believe).

Because it's not actually a struggle between believers and nonbelievers; it's between people who believe what they hear from the cool guy on stage (feelings and vibes) and people who believe what they read.

Even that can get dicey, as illustrated by a recent question posed by my friend Aly (@femlosophy on Substack). Should we (Christians, collectively) have translated the Bible? Are we actually even following the directions left for us?

There are over 450 translations of the Bible in the English language alone. This includes both the universally accepted versions, as well as the controversial ones like The Passion Translation, which has frequently been decried as heretical and/or blasphemous. Even still, it remains popular with many Christians, most especially charismatic congregations. That's a problem, right?

It's the inerrant word of God, but paraphrasing is okay? Even though getting it wrong means roasting in hell for all eternity (as well as everyone else who read and abided by your faulty translation)?

Which of these versions gives a full representation of how we as Christians are meant to think, act, and believe? And which of them are full of shit?

In varying degrees of severity, are they ALL full of shit?

And if they are, why does the well-dressed adulterer and gambling addict at the pulpit think he can tell me what to do and how to live?

I'll give this to the Muslims, they understand version control, and it's prevented a lot of confusion.

Scripture was handed down specifically so that we could continue to be obedient after God stopped speaking to us directly: "Therefore, my beloved, as you have always **obeyed**, not as in my presence only, but now much more in my absence, work out your own salvation with **fear and trembling**." (Philippians 2:12)

The question is, when He says "my beloved" is he talking to ALL humans? Abin Cooper says no. And if we're being honest, so does scripture.

THE UNPLEASANT TRUTH

Modern churches like to gloss over the elements of their own faith that don't square with modern, liberal sensibilities.

The primary tenet of Christianity these days is that Jesus died on the cross for all mankind (Calvinists disagree) and that ALL human life is sacred.

But then you look for biblical justification on the sacredness of all human life, you come up short.

Most often we point to Genesis:

"Let us make mankind in our image, in our likeness." (1:26) and "Whoever sheds man's blood, by man shall his blood be shed; for in the image of God has God made mankind."

So is it all humans whose lives are sacred? Or just the ones who are obedient to His word?

Somewhere along the way, Christianity forgot that "narrow is the path" stuff and decided to become a big tent, one with no standards or requirements, not even the belief in the words right in front of you.

Thus we have the strange spectacle of people declaring themselves atheist whenever they find something in the Bible that goes against their own preferences.

Just because you don't like something doesn't mean it's false.

Like they say, two things can be true at once, and I think Richard B Riddick said it best, in the movie Pitch Black: "You got it all wrong, holy man. I absolutely believe in God. And I absolutely hate the fucker."

Abin Cooper recounts scripture to his own family and asks them regarding God's words and actions, "Does that sound like someone who loves you?"

Without fear and obedience of His Word, the answer to that seems to be no.

I think that's the line that drove Smith away from his original ending.

If Cooper was right about the rapture, right about how FEW would make the cut when the four horsemen descended, then he was right about the poor gay man not having a sacred and valuable life.

He was right that the horny teenage boys deserved to be mowed down by machine guns.

And he was right that the federal agents deserved to have their heads exploded.

Kevin Smith wasn't willing to stand by any of that, so

he changed *Red State*'s ending message to, "Religious fundamentalists bad. And federal agents also bad."

That's a far easier message to stand by, both for the atheist libs he caters to and the Christian conservatives he doesn't.

PART THREE
THE LURKING SICKNESS IN
HUMAN NATURE

CHAPTER 8
THE FEMALE DISPLAY OF PSYCHOPATHY

I HAVE a particular interest in feminine aggression and how women's ways of destruction differ from the masculine baseline of beatings, gunfights, and demolition of infrastructure. The Netflix Marvel shows (now on Disney+) have been universally strong in depicting women as realistic, complicated, and aggressive in uniquely feminine ways.

Heroines like super-powered Jessica Jones and driven Karen Page exemplify these complex feminine qualities, but so too do the female villains — especially the ones who don't realize they're causing harm.

Daredevil season 3 and The Punisher season 2 have an important connection that struck me: They both feature a female psychologist whose overabundance of care for her patient results in great harm being wrought on the populace. I don't think it's a coincidence there is a fair bit of overlap in the writers for these two shows (all 12 writers for Punisher also were part of the team for Daredevil).

FACILITATING MALE VILLAINY

The psychiatrist in Daredevil is brought in to treat a pre-teen Benjamin Poindexter after he accidentally kills his baseball coach with a ricocheting curveball. His therapist, Eileen Mercer, is assigned to treat him, as Dex is a ward of the state.

Eileen is not a stupid woman and is not portrayed as such. She identifies almost immediately that rather than being traumatized, Dex is perfectly fine with his coach's death. She sees that Dex does not love. And he simply doesn't understand why other people do. Dex is a psychopath.

It's what happens after Dex freely admits to her that he killed his coach on purpose that reveals her unintentional destiny to put the general public in danger:

In watching Dex's nonplussed demeanor, Eileen understands immediately he is a psychopath. And instead of recommending he be removed from decent people, she tries to help him. It seems she does this out of love, with the idea that he can be aimed in the right direction. But she's fooling herself. She doesn't aim him anywhere. She teaches him to mimic normal human emotions he doesn't feel, like empathy. She teaches him to hide his absolute disregard for other people behind a structured job and a script for human interaction. Even on her deathbed, he wants to kill her because she is leaving him. She is not meeting his needs.

Even more diabolical is The Punisher's Dr. Krista DuMont, who is assigned to rehabilitate the psyche of rogue assassin Billy Russo after his season one run-in with the Punisher left him in a coma, with amnesia, and devastating scars on his face. Krista's pathological need to "fix"

Billy takes on a different tone than Eileen's relationship with Dex. Not only is Billy a grown man, but also (prior to his scarring) unambiguously handsome. He's also a former Marine Operator and still has the body of a Greek god. Though Krista calls all her patients "wounded birds" and treats them as such, it's not difficult to figure out why she would devote herself so entirely to Billy's recovery. Even after meeting Agent Nadami, the woman Billy seduced and then shot in the head, Krista tells everyone who will listen that Billy is "her patient," is "different now," and "deserves redemption."

Yes, of course he does, you thirsty bitch.

A "HELPING HAND" THAT DESTROYS

But the writers weren't so lazy as to write Krista off as a case of a crush gone bad. Like Eileen, they paint her as The Devouring Mother, an archetype that has been around for centuries. Most laymen have only come to know about it thanks to Jordan Peterson's books and lectures. In explaining the apparent inability for Millennials to deal with any opinions that conflict with their own, overcome even minor adversity, or tolerate ambiguity, he points to the hovering and permissive tendencies of their Gen X and Baby Boomer parents and the proliferation of single mothers.

In doing everything for their children, the devouring mother paints herself as the ultimate caregiver, one who will do anything to help their children. But this willingness comes at a terrible price. As Peterson explains it: "I'll do everything for you to make sure you never leave me."

We see this in both of Marvel's toxic female psychiatrists. Eileen continues to "treat" Dex long after he ages out of the foster care system, telling herself she is helping him keep his psychopathy under control. "You have a moral compass," she tells him. "It just needs to be pointed in the right direction." Of course, she is the one who can do the pointing. Even on her death bed, she is giving him instructions on what type of job to pursue and to continue listening to their session tapes for guidance.

And Krista... there is no professional or ethical boundary she does not cross. And she feels righteous when she does it. She is the arbiter of right and wrong. The only one fit to judge Billy and decide his fate. Anyone else who comes along with a different idea... well, she deals with that as any loving mother would.

A good villain is a key part of any good narrative, whether in book, film, or tv series form. But it is the truly outstanding narratives that feature villains that work as cautionary tales. The ones who show us that fabled road to perdition and the carcasses of good intentions that pave it.

CHAPTER 9
THE VILLAINY OF LACK OF CARE

I MENTIONED the most recent entry into the Scream franchise in my last blog. Part of the reason Wes Craven made Scream 4 (and now other creators have made Scream 5) is that horror, as a genre, has changed significantly since its heyday in the 1970s and 1980s.

When Scream revived the genre for the screen (it never went away in print), it also revived the creativity among screen writers to find new, original ways to horrify and frighten. A welcome addition to the genre was the manifestation of mental illness as the villain in horror and psychological thrillers. Movies like *Hereditary* and The *Babadook terrified* audiences with horrific examinations of grief, while movies like *Melancholia* and *Shutter Island* dispensed with the jump scares and focused on the terror of having your mind and emotions not under your own control.

Some of these excellent films are instances where the mental illness itself is the villain (*Black Swan*), and some are instances where mental illness drives otherwise good people to harm others (*Split*).

2019's *The Lodge* is a masterful, and terrifying, example of both.

More than anything, this film is about unintended consequences and how we don't really "see" other people and the demons they live with.

The first scenes are devoted to a father of two, Richard, telling his wife that he plans to divorce her. He has met someone else and he's like to marry her. The wife, played by Alicia Silverstone, waits for him to leave with the children, and promptly commits suicide.

But this moment of despair is not the subject of the movie. It's just the inciting incident.

Six months later, Richard tells his two children, Mia and Adrian, they will be going to the family's remote winter cabin to spend Christmas... with Grace. The woman he left their mother for. The woman who, in their mind, caused their mother's suicide.

You can see why they'd want revenge, especially Aiden, who tried without luck to comfort his emotionally distraught younger sister, while their father did nothing.

But Grace isn't some airhead their dad met at a bar. She is the only surviving member of a suicide cult, raised under the leadership of a charismatic lunatic who emphasized physical punishment for repentance of sins. He also forced them all to pay the ultimate price for their sins... suicide.

Grace was the only survivor and it's not clear if an adult neglected to poison her like the other children or if she simply declined to kill herself. Richard met her when he wanted to document her story for a book.

When we meet Grace, two important things become clear: 1) She takes prescription medication twice a day without fail, and 2) The children absolutely despise her.

Richard then leaves Grace and the children in the cabin. Alone. And the children will have their revenge.

It's hard to say what Aidan thought would happen when he drugged Grace and hid all her possessions (including her medication).

I can't imagine what this grief-stricken 13-year-old boy thought would happen when he tried to convince a PTSD-afflicted survivor of a death cult that she was indeed already dead, and the three of them were in purgatory.

It's not hard to see where he got the idea. He watched *The Others*, just like I did. And he decided to punish Grace, to make her think she was in purgatory for the sin she had committed against his mother. Against him and his sister.

But he's just a boy. He could not possibly have known what his actions would bring forth.

It is never said what Grace's pills are. But as we see her desperation to find them and her rapid descent into psychotic episodes and fugue states, I suspect they were antipsychotics.

It is only after they see Grace sitting outside in sub-zero temperatures in house clothes (they hid all the coats and shoes), clutching her little dog who froze to death, that they understand they have gone too far.

Aidan wraps a coat around her shoulders and says, "We were just pretending Grace. We're not dead or in purgatory. We were just pretending."

It is far, far too late.

Even if Aidan had read her medication bottle, would he have known what the long word meant? Probably not. If he were older, would he have had a better under-standing that Grace may not view her surviving the cult to be a good thing? I don't know.

The Lodge is marketed as a horror movie and it is

certainly horrifying. But it is ultimately a tragedy of children lashing out in pain, having no idea of the consequences. Because how could they?

It's hard to blame the children, or even Grace's mental illness. After all, if kept under control with medication, therapy, and a support network, she would have been fine. And so would everyone else.

No, if there is a villain in this movie, it is Richard. He divorced his loving and faithful wife for a much younger and prettier woman, expecting his children to just go along with it. He brushed off their grief at their mother's suicide, shoehorning this other woman into their family despite his children's clear opposition.

Then he left them alone in an isolated cabin. With a woman they hated. Who was on antipsychotics.

He knew everything about her experience. He had the footage from the cult, the police reports, everything. He knew exactly how tenuous Grace's grip on reality was. But "it'll be fine."

For Richard, everything will always be fine. Except this time it wasn't. And Richard should have been able to see it coming.

Lord knows, his children didn't.

PART FOUR
GENDER, POWER, AND MORAL ORDER

CHAPTER 10
THE GODZILLA MODEL: HUMANS AS DISEASE

WHEN I WATCHED GODZILLA: King of the Monsters, I was ready for a good time. Yes, I knew the plot might be silly, the writing half-baked. But the cast was wonderful and I love a good monster movie.

However, the plot was not silly. It was... troubling. And to be honest, I'm concerned Godzilla vs. Kong might continue in that same troublesome vein. Let me explain.

The main conflict in the first movie is that scientist Dr. Emma Russell (played by the lovely Vera Farmiga) works with a band of violent eco-terrorists to intentionally awaken all of "the titans," so they might destroy the earth, or at least a good portion of it.

Why, you ask? Because when Godzilla wrecked great portions of US cities, one of her two children died. Her son. As a result of that trauma, she adopted the ideology that Godzilla and the rest of the titans are rising to cleanse the earth of the virus of humans. That the titans are the rightful lords of earth and that they were the original gods of humanity.

In furtherance of this ideology, here is a list of what she did:

- Circumvented the defenses of her own lab and allowed terrorists to shoot and kill dozens of men and women, all of whom Emma knew and worked with.
- Set off explosives to intentionally kill members of the US military and her ex-husband, the father of her children.
- Used her proprietary technology to incite the titans to destroy specific targets, killing thousands, if not hundreds of thousands.
- Gave a speech about humans being a virus and deserving of terrible death, while she and her daughter remain safe from the rampage in a bunker. Hmmm.

Her reasoning seems to be, "my kid died. Now everyone else's kids should die too."

Right now, you may be thinking, "Good. A movie's villain should be complex." But here's the thing...

EMMA IS NEVER PAINTED AS A VILLAIN.

Screen Junkies rightly pointed out in the Honest Trailer that the whole "I'm going to destroy the earth to save it" motivation is so overdone as to be cliche. But as far as I know, this is the first time the writers and producers of the film are actively endorsing it. Why do I know they endorse it? For three specific reasons.

In her monologue, Emma talks about how cities destroyed by the titans were now green utopias, showing footage of trees, flowers, and other greenery growing around the once-grand casinos. Under normal circumstances, this should be a horrible sight. But in the closing shots, there are newspaper headlines flashing across the screen, accompanied by upbeat music:

"New Ecosystem forming in Boston!"

"Air Cleanest Levels Ever in Washington DC!"

Yeah... because everybody is FUCKING DEAD.

Godzilla and at least some of the titans are treated as the heroes in this movie. The humans are really just a framing device. This is brought into stark relief when the team is tracking an injured Godzilla into the depths of the earth. Using an unmanned sub, they find him in the remains of a very ancient city — older than ancient Egypt, older than the Sumerians. So what do they do when they find this treasure, this great trove of knowledge of our species?

They. Blow it. Up. With a nuke.

Because Godzilla needed a hit of radiation to bring him back to full power. These men and women of science just blew all the evidence of a pre-historical advanced civilization to hell. To save a monster.

And finally, Emma was given a hero's death. She got the dramatic quip and everything. She had a heartwarming reunion with her husband where they searched for their daughter together. She got to stand up and be praised for giving her life to lead the soon-to-be critical-mass monster away from the rest of the group. And then she got to go out like a boss. Everything about her character arc painted her as a sympathetic character, a good mother who had the right idea, but went a little overboard.

For any one of her actions in the list above, Emma deserved to be given a traitor's death. She did not deserve a hug from the man she tried to kill, forgiveness from the daughter she deceived and brainwashed, or the opportunity to bring about the new "cleansed" world she imagined.

The hundreds of thousands of deaths she is personally responsible for are never brought up.

Some of the people most influential in our culture are getting to a weird place. Some broadcast to the world that they refuse to have children because of climate change, despite the fact that their country has below-replacement birth rates. And some people shoot up the city of Dayton because "humanity is a disease."

We know internet enclaves like 4-Chan have a strong nihilistic streak. But are we really in a place where those ideas will be present in our blockbusters? I sincerely hope not.

I hope this was a one-off, even a mistake. I hope those BS headlines at the end of the movie were a set-up for Godzilla vs. Kong, a sequel that will return us to a vision of heroic humans fighting monsters to save the people they love. I hope it makes monster movies fun again.

CHAPTER 11
PRACTICAL MAGIC AND USING MEN FOR SPERM

THE PHENOMENON of men who overtly despise women yet compulsively seek sex and admiration from them is well commented-upon. Shrewd veterans of the dating hellscape can spot such men at a distance.

It's only recently—and by recent, I mean in the past 5 years or so—that the female version of this phenomenon has gotten any attention. At least, negative attention. But it's always been with us, and the destruction that comes in its wake is far worse that harsh words and hurt feelings.

In 1998, the movie *Practical Magic* was released and immediately beloved of almost every woman and girl. It was a witchy, girl-power dramedy that hit all the right notes. So right, in fact, that most of us overlooked the troubling inciting incident.

Young Sally Owens and her sister Jillian are raised by their aunts after being orphaned. All the Owens women are witches. They're born that way. They are also subject to a curse: Any man who genuinely loves an Owens woman is fated to die.

As such, when Sally and Jillian grown up, they are

careful not to fall in love. Though Jullian has plenty of use for men.

Sally (played by Sandra Bullock) lives a solitary life into early adulthood, until one day, she suddenly runs off to the hardware store to accept a date with the cute clerk who's been making eyes at her. She doesn't know why. She is compelled to his side.

But Michael, after giving Sally two daughters, is hit by a truck and dies.

Sally is utterly destroyed and goes to the see the aunts, demanding they bring him back. It's only then she realizes why she ran to the hardware store that day.

> Jet: "It was just a little push… You wanted so much to be happy. We never expected that you'd truly love him."
> Sally: "Well, I did. And I want him back!"

They put a spell on her. Their own niece, to drive her into the arms of a man. They knew he would die as a result. Maybe they thought Sally wouldn't love him. But they knew HE would love HER. And die for it.

Why would they do something so wicked?*

We don't get a clear answer in the actual film, but a *Vice* article (accurately) speculated why the aunts would perform magic to spur Sally into a relationship:

> *Why do the aunts care if she falls in love? The same reason anyone's family prods them towards heterosexual life choices: procreation. The curse appears to set in just after an Owens woman has time to bear two daughters, a new version of herself*

---

* This only refers to the movie version of *Practical Magic*. The book has some sizeable differences, including the characterization of the aunts.

and her sister, one sensible brunette and one wild redhead. How else would the curse live on for another generation? The curse isn't just that any man an Owens woman loves will die. The curse is that Owens women will love men, period. - Natalie Adler

Despite its valid motive for the aunt's horrific behavior, the Vice article goes on to make the preposterous claim that the Owens family curse was created for a particular reason: "… to save the women from male violence."

In other words, he had it coming.

The problem, of course, is that this is nonsense.

JUSTIFYING FEMALE VIOLENCE AGAINST MEN

In the movie, and in the book that inspired it, the curse was plainly a reaction from Maria Owens, the matriarch of the Owens family, after being betrayed by her love.

Maria had an affair with John Hathorne, a witch-hunter, which resulted in the birth of her daughter Faith. Her heart was shattered at being abandoned by the man she loved. Pain turned to anger. As it so often does.

Rejection can bring on a type of madness. A spiral into man hatred.

"He left me because he is a man. Men are cruel. He used me for sex and dropped me when I wasn't convenient! I need to protect other women. Not just from him, but from them all!"

It doesn't seem to matter what men say or how they act. The story heartbroken women tell themselves stays the same.

That's why the Vice writer twisted herself into knots

trying to make it sound like "all this could have been avoided if men weren't such meanies."

It's why women laughed and cheered en masse at Lorena Bobbit for chopping off her husband's penis.

And why, years later, Sharon Osborne and other female tv hosts cackled live on network television about a similar case of male sexual mutilation.

"He was a cheater. He was abusive. Probably a child molester. They all are."

This manner of thinking is not just for out-of-touch Hollywood types of even women who have experienced abuse. It has infected us all.

ART IMITATES LIFE

There was nothing unique about real-life murderer Kathleen Dorsett. A middle-class, Midwestern girl. An elementary school teacher.

She did well in school, had friends, met a nice man, married him, and had a baby.

But then (stop me if you've heard this one), she "just wasn't happy." Kathleen got increasingly short with her husband Stephen, pushy, and demeaning. Finally, she filed for divorce, demanding full custody of their daughter.

According to interviews with Stephen's friends (as seen on both Dateline and Snapped), Kathleen was both shocked and enraged that Stephen had that gall to demand shared custody of their child.

"She used me as a sperm donor," he told his friends. There was no other explanation that made sense to him. She'd been the ideal wife right up until she had the baby. And it wasn't due to his negligence. He took great pains to be hands-on in parenting, which seemed to make Kathleen even angrier.

A longtime friend of Stephen's speculated she never loved him, that the plan all along was to have a baby, thinking that Stephen, being a man, would willingly walk away from his child.

When he refused, she lured him to his death (with the help of her parents... oh my God) and set his body on fire.

Because this was HER baby. Who did this MAN think he was to imagine he had any rights to his own child?

And it wasn't until Kathleen and her parents were charged that anyone in her social circle batted an eye. Kathleen sneering cruelty toward Stephen, her willful defiance of court orders to let him see his own child—all of it was shrugged off by every woman she knew.

"Yeah, my ex tries to control me through the kids too," one of them said (on television, no less).

It's baby rabies turned up to 11.

But why? Why marry a man you don't love just to use him as a sperm donor?

My sister in Christ, you can buy sperm on the internet *right now*. You had a job. With benefits. You had involved parents who were willing to provide child care. Why trick a man into thinking you loved him only to drive him from his family once you had what you wanted?

It's gross. Respectability politics run amok. These women view men as so disposable that they think nothing of using them for an easily gained body fluid, all so they don't have to take on the title of "single mom."

Divorce is no longer shameful. But being a baby mama is. So they do the logical thing: destroy a man's life to protect their own image. After all, "he had it coming."

I don't want to be controversial here, but it seems to me

that men are people. They have feelings. They have souls. They have hopes and dreams and love their children and love their wives.

They have pride as well, just like we do. Show me a man who stays with a wife who treats him like shit and I'll show you a man who fears the stink of failure above all things.

A man is a lot more than a roof fixer and sperm donor. Be sure to remember that when you take pains to ensnare one.

They're not so impervious to heartbreak as you've been led to believe.

CHAPTER 12
A WOMAN'S PLACE

IT WOULD BE AN EASIER life if I could somehow not believe in God.

People who think humans are merely highly intelligent, sparsely-haired primates can explain the way women are and what we're for any number of ways, coming to a far more flattering conclusion than I have.

But if you believe in an omniscient, all-seeing creator who formed humans in His own image with great care and purpose, then it simply isn't enough to shrug and laugh. "Women, amiright?"

I am not in a good place as I write this, and it was probably a mistake to think deeply about what anonymous males on Twitter say about women. But there's just so many of them and they all say such similar things.

And what they say so closely matches what I have seen myself. Maybe the bile they spew bears closer examination, even if it hurts.

Even if you end the night with Googling: "Catholicism, do women have souls?"

YOU KNOW YOU LIKE IT

We really do like it, don't we? Being stepped on. When you think about it, there simply isn't another explanation when you look at the global, historical behavior patterns of what we seek out and what we tolerate, even after the thrill is long gone.

From a Christian perspective, submission and obedience is the right and proper way of the female, meaning the role of the male is one of dominion. Anyone raised in any kind of Christian church knows that. It's not even controversial.

□ WE ARE CALLED as women to affirm and encourage men as they seek to express godly masculinity, and to honor and support God-ordained male leadership in the home and in the church.[10]

□ MARRIAGE, as created by God, is a sacred, binding, lifelong covenant between one [biologically-born] man and one [biologically-born] woman.[11]

□ WHEN WE RESPOND humbly and appropriately to God-ordained leadership in our homes and churches, we demonstrate a noble submission that honors God's Word and reflects Christ's obedience to the will of His Father.[12]

□ SELFISH INSISTENCE on personal rights is contrary to the spirit of Christ who humbled Himself, took on the form of a servant, and laid down His life for us.[13]

From Revive Our Hearts, a Christian women's ministry

Men lead, women follow.

Men give, women receive.

Men impregnate, women become pregnant.

It's not the dynamic I'm questioning. It's the reasoning behind it, mostly because of the sexual aspect of the male-female relationship, less so for the child-rearing part of it.

The sex, the desire for it (primarily from men) is the main driver for relationships to even exist.

There have been so many men who have said right out loud that if it were not for the sex—and their all-consuming thirst for it—they would have nothing to do with us at all.

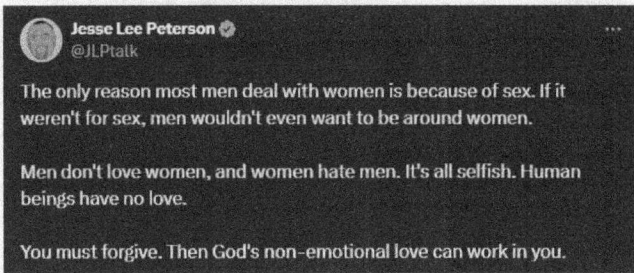

And yet we still seek them out, looking for the one man who likes us, actually. It sounds simple. But it's not.

Because we have desires of our own.

A healthy sexual dynamic between a man and woman will generally include his desire to possess or conquer her, and her desire to be possessed or conquered. However, this desire is very specific... he wants to conquer a woman who wants to be conquered by HIM, and she wants to be conquered by a specific man because she believes he deserves her. Their desires align.

The degenerate man desires to conquer a very specific category of woman: the woman who rejects him.

He has no interest in the woman who desires him. He has no desire to be worthy of anything or anyone. He delights in the core practice of his degeneracy: imposition. It is seeing her repulsed but helpless is what excites him because he is a sadist. That is the core of male sexual degeneracy: sadism. (@Dvorstone on X)

That sounds so nice. And it makes sense.

The majority of men, after all, do not prefer to buy prostitutes and disdain those who subscribe to an Only-

Fans cam-whore. That's not a conquest; it's a transaction. It's not manly.

And deep down, they know the hooker doesn't really want them, cheapening the experience even more. The conquering is only fun, only worth it, if she wants him. If she *wants* what he plans to do to her.

The degradation of women during sex is baked into the process, a fact that neither men nor women likes to admit. We all agree on the lie that actions like expelling body fluids onto someone's face and/or into their mouth, pinning a person so they are immobile, and sticking foreign objects into someone's throat until retching occurs are not behaviors indicating respect or esteem.

They are actions of domination, of destruction--yet they are actions that women desire.

But *why* do we want it? What exactly went into our construction to make us want, NEED, to be ruled?

It sure as hell wasn't sugar and spice.

What is it that makes us, in the millions, read books that feature these tropes as a means of sexual arousal:

- Stalking (Hello, <u>Haunting Adeline</u>)
- Cheating/infidelity
- Serial killer
- Nonconsensual/Dubious consent
- Bully
- Mafia
- BDSM
- Knife play (seriously wtf)
- Kidnapping (Oh, hey <u>365</u>)
- Primal play
- Somnophilia

Those are the most popular tropes in dark romance, something I've talked about before.

I have to. I'm compelled to talk about it. Mostly because I like it too and I don't understand why.

THE SIXTH DAY

It would be a mean thing, a cruel thing, to make a creature for servitude while giving them a drive for conquest.

Luckily, it seems the Almighty spared us this cruelty. He even gave us an inborn psychological defense mechanism against the subjugation—arousal at acts of domination.

As I said in the beginning, things would be easier if I were an atheist, or could even fathom being so.

I know there are other religions with other origin stories. But they don't count. Not to me. Sorry.

Christians, Muslims, and Jews know that God Almighty made Adam first. And was pretty pleased with what he made:

> 26 And God said, Let us make man in our image, after our likeness: and let him have dominion over the fish of the sea, and over the fowl of the air, and over the cattle, and over all the earth, and over every creeping thing that creepeth upon the earth.
>
> 27 So God created man in his own image, in the image of God created he him; male and female created he them. (Genesis 1:26-27, KJV)

Now verse 27 is a little ambiguous in who exactly was made in His image, as "man" can mean humanity as a whole.

But I don't think that blessing applies to women. I really don't. Mostly because of the reason Eve came about in the first place:

> 20 And Adam gave names to all cattle, and to the fowl of the air, and to every beast of the field; **but for Adam there was not found an help meet for him.**
>
> 21 And the LORD God caused a deep sleep to fall upon Adam, and he slept: and he took one of his ribs, and closed up the flesh instead thereof;
>
> 22 And the rib, which the LORD God had taken from man, made he a woman, and brought her unto the man.
>
> 23 And Adam said, This is now bone of my bones, and flesh of my flesh: she shall be called Woman, because she was taken out of Man. (Genesis 2:20-22, KJV)

She wasn't designed in her own right, to fulfill her own purpose.

She was designed to help him with his.

Nothing ambiguous about that at all.

MEN: LOOK AFTER YOUR PETS AND WOMEN

The ordained superior nature of men would relegate women to the same or slightly higher category as animals. Men are charged with being good custodians of the earth, including the animals within it. They are also commanded by the Almighty in multiple passages (mostly in the Old Testament) to care for their women. It is his solemn duty to protect, guide, and teach her. Even into adulthood. Because she is less, even on a spiritual level.

I. As to the first question, it is evident that both man and woman are the image of God in as far as both possess the same human nature. The text Gen. i. 27, affirms this explicitly; and in Gen. ii. 18–20, the woman is distinguished from the animals as being a help like unto or meet for man—that is, of the same nature.

It is, nevertheless, true that of man alone Scripture says, directly and formally, that he is made to the likeness of God. Hence St. Paul teaches : " The man indeed ought not to cover his head, because he is the image and glory of God ; but the woman is the glory of the man. For the man is not of the woman, but the woman of the man. For the man was not created for the woman, but the woman for the man " (1 Cor. xi. 7–9). Woman, then, having received human nature only mediately through man, and to be a helpmate to man, is not an image of God in the same full sense as man. Woman, considered as wife—that is, in a position of subjection and dependence, —is in no wise an image of God, but rather a type of the relation which the creature bears to the Creator and Lord.

From Wilhelm and Scannel's Manual of Catholic Theology

Following the pattern of feminine inferiority, Irenaeus considered women generally as the cause of sin and the subsequent alienation of humanity from God. However, he emphasised that Mary's piety was far more important than Eve's curse. For him, the 'virgin Mary' has redeemed all women from the sinful innate lust of the female gender (Sawyer 1996:157). After the same pattern, Clement of Alexandria proposed that God took away the weakness of Adam and used it to create Eve. For this reason, he considered women as weak, limited, passive, 'castrated', 'immature', 'licentious, and unjust' (Ide 1984:66).[*]

I have no insight into Clement of Alexandria, and am

---

[*] Owusu-Gyamfi, Clifford, & Dei, Daniel. (2022). Tertullian's moral

not so glib as to ask, "Who hurt you, bro?" I can only point out that it is somewhat hypocritical to accuse women of lust and licentiousness, when men obviously suffer such things with far greater intensity.

But in all honesty, men's lust and their unslakeable thirst for sex are not an accident.

Like the saying goes, it's not a bug; it's a feature.

As women were made to crave our own degradation and subordination, men were made to crave dishing it out.

Why does man do anything? Why does he create, build, and innovate?

In crass terms, for pussy.

It's well known that men are perfectly happy to live like this:

Disgusting to behold

So why do they spend so much time trying to get rich? Why the fancy cars, the bling-y watches? Why the too-tight high-water pants that cost $1500? (You all look ridiculous, by the way).

For chicks. They're signaling their wealth to attract women. Everything they do is to get girls. Including building the civilization and infrastructure we currently enjoy.

theology on women and the accusation of misogyny. *Verbum et Ecclesia,*
43(1), 1-8. https://dx.doi.org/10.4102/ve.v43i1.2384

Camille Paglia said, "If civilization had been left in female hands, we would still be living in grass huts."

And she's right. Women make a house a home. But it's men who build the house in the first place.

Men *only* build for pussy and progeny (their legacy). Remove the promise or even the possibility of either, and they turn into destroyers.

That innate drive within them will seek to conquer one way or another. Which is where we come in.

We were created to make them better. Not ourselves. We only matter in terms of what we improve in them.

Men were made to be leaders, to be BETTER than us. So why aren't they? Why are they stagnating globally and, in the West, getting worse?

Is that our fault too?

In a way... Yes.

WHAT TO DO WITH THE MEN

In pursuing greatness for ourselves, on a societal level we have left great swaths of men feeling the promise of pussy slip away.

Niku
@officialniku

Modern men have to work 5x harder than their grandfathers for women 20x worse than what their grandmothers were.

It's called hoeflation and it's destroying western men's desires to be providers
and protectors.

10:01 AM · Jul 5, 2022

It's not just because we're sleeping with guys outside of marriage. It's also the access we all have on a global level. A pretty girl need only start an Instagram page to be solicited by wealthy older men who will give her the type of lifestyle the nice boy down the street never could.

There's also the issue that we, as a whole, are getting fatter and uglier. American food is borderline poison, throwing our hormones out of whack. Just look at the skyrocketing instances of PCOS. And we dress like shit.

And many of us are mean. Rude. Unwelcoming. It's a societal model fed to us for three generations that if you want to be a strong woman, that means being a relentless bitch.

Men, despite their unyielding sex drive, are ceasing to be interested.

The juice ain't worth the squeeze as the old saying goes.

Men perform more and better if they receive female admiration and attention, even if no sex is involved.

Chinese tech companies reportedly hiring 'cheerleaders' to motivate programmers

Cheerleader duties said to include buying breakfast, chit-chat and Ping-Pong

A WOMAN'S CALLING?

Many women, even those in the church, chafe at the term "helpmeet." The definition is benign—a helpful companion or partner—but the reality of our nature doesn't fit with our current "main character syndrome" society.

It also reframes the common male complaint of "nagging" or "withholding sex."

Based on the wreck and ruin I see around me, it seems both of those things are not only in order, but my duty to apply. Maybe the gold diggers are onto something, fulfilling their female role in the best way they know how.

Our job is to nag you. To shame you. To hold sex over your head like a fucking death sentence. Oh, baby wants a blowjob? Then I guess baby better build me a fucking

95

sewage system. Oh, baby wants to pass his genes onto the next generation of men? Then I guess baby better get a job that pays six figures and gives me health insurance.

Because if my entire reason for being is to bring you to your highest form—to encourage and cheer you into excellence while taking none for myself—then it stands to reason that it is my solemn, sacred duty to civilize you and to nag you either into your grave or into your highest form. Not sorry.

And before you red pill boys chime in with recommendations based on non-western marriage practices, I invite you to look at how those societies function.

Look at the societies where men only need purchase young (very young) virgins from their fathers. They don't need to earn the affection and loyalty of women. They just need to buy them, trade for them, and maybe impress the girl's father. Maybe.

Pakistan, Afghanistan, FLDS communities in the US...

They don't do a lot of building, innovating, and creating. Do they? They aren't known for high IQs. Or even physical attractiveness. Mormons in general are often strikingly good looking. But if you look specifically at the Fundamentalist ones... the same can't be said.

Do you aspire to THIS, gentlemen?

Striving for a worthy woman is what makes you what you are.

We each have our own nature to provide an incentive structure to the other. This incentive structure is to draw out the finest in the individual and, on a wider scale, the society.

Yes, that does include a hierarchy and doing what you're supposed to doesn't automatically guarantee you the top-shelf prize.

- Only the highest tier of men (looks/money/swag) have access to the most beautiful women.
- Only the most beautiful and appealing women get to be stay-at-home wives to a rich man.

Them's the breaks. The rest of us have to sweeten the pot with acts of service.

He needs to be emotionally present and fun to be around, at least most of the time. He needs to engage in non-sexual intimacy so she feels attractive and valued. He needs to be an involved father and participate in the household maintenance.

She needs to make his doctor's appointments and dinner. She needs to raise the children and be mindful of what their teachers are telling them. She needs to maintain her appearance and have sex with him regularly.

These are the rules—the give and take that keep the relationship and our very lives on an even keel.

After so many years of being lied to, it seems wrong, dirty even, to think about willfully subordinating ourselves.

But deep down, it feels right.

That's why we seek it out in fiction, a safe way to play act what we know is the truth:

Men were made in His image. Not women.

We were only ever spare parts.

CHAPTER 13
THE SHOCKING INGRATITUDE FOR GOOD MEN

ON A RECENT PODCAST, I spilled my little secret that I, like most women, spent my early 20s in a state of liberal feminism. Nothing as extreme as you see today, of course, but the classic narratives were all there: Men were violent, women were victims. Men were mean, women were reactive. This was the unassailable mental model I had of inter-gender relations. It was how I was raised, how I was taught, and frankly, what I saw with my own eyes.

I was lucky enough to find the *one* awesome guy with a rockin' bod before the other girls snatched him up. "I got the only good one, ladies! Pack it up!"

Silly, I know. Much of my ideological shift away from feminist nonsense came slowly, over many years. But my first and biggest step came shortly after I got married.

When my new husband's coworker was murdered by his wife.

Joe Stutzman was not good friends with my husband. Actually, they didn't get along AT ALL. But when Joe's wife <u>asked several teen boys</u> to stab him to death in his own damn house, it hit both of us hard.

Hubs felt guilty about his last words with Joe being in anger. He also wondered if he should have told someone about the screaming phone calls he overheard while deployed. Husbands and wives fighting was common. Deployments are stressful. But Joe's angry phone calls were different, and Hubs wasn't sure he'd made the right call not to mention it to anyone.

I also felt guilty, but for different reasons. My guilt stemmed from the fact that upon hearing that Brandy had murdered him, my first thought was, "I guess he was abusive."

MEN AS VILLAINS

It wasn't long after Joe was stabbed to death in his home that the truth came out. After all, they always look at the wife first. And Brandy hadn't done a very good job of covering her tracks.

1. She had loud, outrageous parties at the house whenever Joe was deployed (usually 4 months at a time). Parties with men.
2. She did not work and but spent Joe's money like a coke-addled sailor.
3. Joe had been talking about divorcing her with some regularity prior to his most recent deployment.
4. There WAS abuse in the Stutzman house, but it was Brandy who was the abuser.

None of these facts would ever have occurred to me in a million years, even at the advanced age of 28. Even though I had been cruelly bullied by girls in school (never boys). Even though I had my ass handed to me in the Marines by some girl from Baltimore (for no reason).

The only time I've ever had my belongings stolen was also another girl.

I knew damn well how mean girls could be, how spiteful and vengeful. But those bad girls were always viewed as the exception.

While bad men were the rule.

Men were the problem. And if wives were violent or mean or lazy, the men were at fault. Always.

Until…

His name was Joe Stutzman

THE RED FLAGS MEN SEE, BUT ACCEPT

Many years later, the whole ugly story would be featured on an episode of *Snapped*. By then, I was watching true crime shows religiously. Seeing such a familiar face pop up on my screen was jarring, shocking. But not nearly as shocking as how much more I found out about Brandy thanks to the show. How wrong I had been about her…

Deadly Women had already been airing for 5 years at the time of Joe's murder and *Snapped* had been on for 6. At that time, I hadn't seen either of them. Both shows were dedicated solely to female murderers. And there are just SO MANY of them. Far from my assumption that female murderers like Susan Smith (child murderer) and Brynn Hartman (actor Phil Hartman's murderer wife) were rare one-offs, I could see now that they were common as dandelions.

And no, actually. It wasn't their victims' fault. They didn't deserve what they got.

Gambling addiction was a common reason for women murdering their husbands. The women stole from their family or their family's business and, when they were caught (or about to be) they killed their husbands.

Another one was entitlement. "I deserve more than this! Give me more! (or I'll kill you and spend your life insurance on the life I DESERVE).

Brandy's was pure mercenary greed. "I'll give you sex (at first) and a child. In return, I'll spend all your money, do whatever I want with whoever I want, and treat you like crap. Sound good? It doesn't? Okay, well here's three teen boys to break into your house. And then your life insurance will pay for my continued partying."

It should be noted that Brandy was a juggalo, which I didn't know until *Snapped* told me. But Joe did. Living like that is the reddest of flags. Yet Joe chose her and stayed with her longer than was wise. Why?

Even without knowing her lifestyle, I admit to being baffled by their relationship. She isn't even cute. Why would Joe put up with her?

Seeing an average guy with a big-titty smoke wagon who ends up killing him, you kinda get it. He felt lucky to have her and put up with abusive and outrageous behavior. But this cow? This pug-faced tomato-bodied deviant? Bro, why?

I'm not a psychiatrist and I won't pretend to be some

kind of man whisperer. But given my own husband's life matched Joe's pretty closely, I can speculate.

A man goes to a war zone and uses his aircraft expertise, making gobs of money. What does he want when he comes home? Stability, comfort. A woman to welcome him, to show him affection and appreciation, a healthy child who looks up to Daddy for his hard work and bravery. He wants something to make the hardship worth it.

So she's having trouble leaving her old life behind… we'll work through it.

So she still has a poverty mindset and isn't responsible with the budget… we can work through that.

Better to work at the relationship than start from scratch, right? Especially with being deployed half the year. Especially with the threat of alimony and child support and hardly ever seeing your child hanging over your head.

The saddest realization is that Joe lost his life specifically because he was a good man.

I spend a lot of time suppressing the urge to drag younger Red Pill boys to the sink and wash their mouth out with liquid Dial (the most disgusting of soaps). But I can't argue with their anger at how the deck is stacked against them.

Girls have been getting away with egregious ass shit and it's right and good that young men are now being taught to look out for their own interests.

Because if you don't, if you accept the feminist stance that "Men will take what they're given and be grateful" you may find out that picking wrong can have deadly consequences for men too.

CHAPTER 14
THE BOYS SEASON 1: UNAPOLOGETIC MASCULINITY

"WHITE MEN ARE NICE... *until they're not.*"

I have no idea where the quote above comes from. Perhaps it doesn't come from any particular place at all. It's just a sentence that feels like a quote because it's so damn true.

The Boys had so much promise in its first season, a genuinely exciting explosion into the streaming world. Though based on a UK graphic novel, Amazon's adaptation is very much its own narrative, one that ended up being a full-blown meditation on the modern western male, specifically the white variety. It does this with a powerful contrast between the two leads, Hughie Campbell and Billy Butcher.

(At the time of writing this, only the first season had aired. If you follow the show, you know what direction it went in. Like Game of Thrones, let's try to remember the good times, shall we?)

Hughie is the typical white millennial male who we can assume is of Irish derivation. He's passive, indecisive, almost willfully unsuccessful, though funny and kind. He knows he is capable of more, but mustering up the courage to ask his perfectly reasonable boss for a well-deserved raise is just too hard. Certainly moving out of his dad's apartment is way out of his league, even though his lovely girlfriend/fiancé is encouraging him to do his part to kickstart their life together.

All that changes as he holds his girlfriend's hands... and she explodes into a mist of blood, bone, and gore. It happens so fast that Hughie does not immediately understand what's just happened.

A superhero, capable of fantastic speeds, has just run right through her. The slick, handsome young man offers a weak apology, with the girl's blood still on his face. "Sorry, man. I can't stop." And in a blink, he is gone, leaving Hughie standing there, still holding his girlfriend's hands, the only part of her body that was not reduced to pulp.

In this world, superheroes are fawned over, believed to be chosen by God. They are also protected (owned) by a powerful corporation called Voight, which sends a smarmy lawyer to Hughie's house to pay him off. A settlement, they call it.

When he's offered the money, being told this is generous since Robin wasn't his wife, he imagines himself reaching across the table and smashing this smug bastard's face into the table. But what he actually says is: "Let me think about it." He makes noise about turning down the money, but even his loving father says what is true: "You never had any fight in you."

But then, while he is doing his bullshit job, in walks Billy Butcher, the absolute antithesis of Hughie. Billy is bearded, swaggering, and British. Not the "afternoon tea" type of British. The *Lock, Stock, and Two Smoking Barrels* type of British. In truth, actor Karl Urban doesn't quite manage to banish his native New Zealand accent in his portrayal of Billy, but that just makes his performance even more rugged.

I say the show is aptly named because *The Boys* is full-octane testosterone, like the Schwarzenegger movies of old. Shirtless men standing in front of tables full of guns, a cigarette hanging from the lip and swirls of body hair exactly where they should be. No waxing, smoothie-drinking nu-males here. The contrast between Billy, Frenchie, and Mother's Milk (MM) with Hughie is stark... but not mean-spirited. It is worth noting that MM is the only man of color on the team and also the only well-adjusted one. Veteran, husband, father, inspirer of wayward youth... Hughie can see right away that MM is a good man, one to be trusted. He can also see that Billy, despite his swagger, is not.

Drawn into the world of hunting superheroes (supes, as they are called) as revenge for his dead girlfriend, it doesn't take Hughie long to notice something off with Billy. His recklessness. His utter glee when Hughie, against all odds, kills his first Supe. It wasn't the man who killed Robin, so why is Billy so elated? What drives him to do this?

We find out soon enough and it's a similar revenge story to Hughie, but much darker and not at all tempered by the sweetness in Hughie's soul. The Supes are horrendous people (mostly), but is Billy any different?

The Boys is a masterful study in men: What motivates them, what bonds them together... and what they fear. Hughie discovers who he is by actually standing up and saying no more. No, I am not okay with a whole class of people being allowed to kill innocents without consequence. I am not okay with being lied to and my government accepting bribes at the expense of their own people. I am not okay. And I, as a man, will do something.

Dr. Jordan Peterson, in giving advice to aimless young men, says to pick up the heaviest thing you can and carry it as far as you can. Life without a purpose can only lead to tragedy. And for Hughie, this advice works. It focuses his drive and his good character sees him through. Billy... not so much. You see, he didn't pick up the weight on his shoulders. It was dropped on him. And he has allowed his mission to become all-consuming, ignoring every signpost along the way that he is on the wrong path.

Billy is what happens when we let a narrative, an ideology, drive our actions, instead of seeing what is actually there. The angry white man who only listens to the stories in his own head instead of hearing what the people around him are saying. He certainly doesn't listen to Hughie.

The last scene of Season 1 is the most targeted kick in the balls I have ever seen. The fear and insecurity that plagues men (ALL men) and drives them to do some of the worst things to the people they claim to love is used as a weapon against Billy, showing him in one devastating scene how wrong he was about absolutely everything.

As a longtime comic book fan, I loved this show. Loved how they turned the tropes we know on their head. As much as I love the X-Men, I think as we become adults we understand that people with so much power over others rarely use it in magnanimous fashion. *The Boys* may not be the heroes we wanted. But they are the heroes we deserve.

PART FIVE
POWER, JUSTICE, AND OBLIGATION

CHAPTER 15
PARADISE REQUIRES VIOLENCE

FURIOSA IS the prequel to *Mad Max: Fury Road* that no one asked for but was actually good… and truthful.

The movie opens with Furiosa as a young girl living in a green, beautiful place, foraging for apples with another young girl when the sound of motorbikes alerts her to the presence of intruders. We know from watching *Fury Road* that this paradise is one small patch of plenty in a vast wasteland, one that must be kept secret.

Were the men on motor bikes to be allowed to live, they would report back to the other men about this paradise, this place of abundance. And like a swarm of locusts, they would tear through it until nothing remained.

Furiosa knows this, and so does her mother. And together, they endure horrible suffering to keep the secret.

That's the thing about any paradise or utopia. It can only exist for a few. Let the masses in, and it will just turn into hell.

THE TYRANNY OF "SHOULD"

Just like the motorbike-riding marauders, our real world is full of people who see something they want and decide that means the owner or resident of that thing should then give it to them.

This unfortunately large cohort of humanity believes that "I want" is a perfect synonym for "You should."

- "I see you have a house that you only occupy for half the year. I want that house. You should give it to me."
- "I see you have money that you've earned through commerce. I want more money than I have. You should give me yours so I can pay off my debts."
- "I see you have large, bouncing breasts. I want to satisfy my arousal. You should hold still while I grab them, perhaps while calling you names."

The foregone conclusion that we must all defend what is precious in order to preserve and protect it has somehow become lost. There are certain ideologies that have the flip-side of the coin when it comes to "should." Specifically, that we "should" be able to preserve our little paradise without lifting a finger.

That other people "should" do the right thing and leave us be.

"Women should be able to walk down the street buck naked without being harassed!"

This nonsensical assertion completely ignores human nature as well as applying some weird revisions to history, insisting that in times past, men were better, more refined, and would never stoop to leering or groping (or worse).

Of course this is ridiculous. The Victorian era is often mentioned as a time when men were gentlemen.

If you'll recall the Virgina Woolf masterpiece *Orlando*, when our main character inexplicably switches from being a young man to a young woman, Orlando is startled at the fact that he (now she) can't walk anywhere alone. When Orlando attempts to do so, random gentlemen sprint to her, offering the protection of their arm.

Women did not walk alone. Not ladies anyway. It was understood they needed protection and the men were duty-bound to provide it.

Those same Victorian gentlemen carried canes as part of their attire. Or long, heavy-handled umbrellas even when it wasn't raining.

Do you think they had a hard time walking? That there was some outbreak of polio?

No.

They carried these accessories to beat brigands about the neck and shoulders should they dare accost a lady or attempt thievery.

Duels were also a thing—first with swords, then with pistols—when a man stepped out of bounds.

It wasn't that people were better back then; they most certainly weren't. It's just that there were consequences. The people knew that in order to preserve what was precious, violence *would* be required.

Somewhere we lost that.

GOOD FENCES, GOOD NEIGHBORS

This two-pronged "should" war has dissolved the formerly high-trust society I grew up in, and it's not something I've taken to.

I rather liked living in a high-trust society, one where private property and bodily autonomy were just a given. Not everyone had that blessing in their youth, never knew what it felt like to leave your front door unlocked, as no one would ever dare enter without knocking and awaiting for an invitation.

Some women have never experienced the ability to walk outside their front door in short-shorts and a tank top, knowing that if a man stopped to talk to you, it was for a nice catch-up, an inquiry into your grades, and a request to tell your father he said hello.

The "should" people very often never experienced that, whether raised here or abroad, and they don't think you ever deserved it in the first place. They also get palpably angry when we lament its absence now. They call our collective memory of the safety of the 80s and 90s a delusion.

But it wasn't a delusion. It was just that there were expectations baked into society. We didn't have to say to each other:

- This is my house, not yours. You have no right to enter or approach without my permission.
- I am a person; my body is my own. You have no right to touch it unless I say so.
- This is my country, not yours. You are not entitled to what we have simply because you covet it for yourself.

We didn't have to say these things because individually and as a society, it was made plain there would be consequences for violating our sovereign personal and property rights.

It's not enough to build a paradise. That very act is an invitation for others to come and take it for themselves. We have always known this, and yet our comfortable, too-long prosperity has convinced a powerful few that it is enough to use calming words and the occasional offering to the wolves baying at the door.

It isn't. It will never be.

The carrot is all well and good to motivate good behavior among the in-group.

But it's the stick that makes us safe from the outside.

CHAPTER 16
LET'S KILL ALL THE CHILDREN, SHALL WE?

I'M NOT sure there's ever been a society with such pervasive animus between the old and their progeny. Traditionally, the goal of every generation has been to make a world better for their children, to teach, toil, and sacrifice to give the youth a leg up. But no more.

Scroll through social media and you'll find countless examples of older Americans – particularly Baby Boomers – expressing open disdain for younger generations while simultaneously hoarding the very resources that could help them succeed.

The statistics are staggering: many older Americans are sitting on millions in home equity while their adult children struggle to afford rent. They're refusing to retire from jobs that could provide career advancement for younger workers. They're spending lavishly on luxury cruises and expensive hobbies while their adult children ask for help with student loans or down payments, only to be told they need to "work harder" and "stop being entitled."

Most disturbing of all, surveys show that many older Americans are intentionally spending down their wealth to avoid leaving inheritances. "I earned my way in this world; they can do the same."

This isn't universal, of course. Many boomers have always and continue to sacrifice for their kids and grandkids. But on the wider scale, boomers have created a system where young people can't afford homes, can't save for retirement, can't start families, and then they mock those same young people for failing to achieve traditional markers of success.

It all leads to yet another piece of dystopian fiction that is starting to look strangely prescient.

1984 and *Brave New World* get cited all the time as being true to life, but it wasn't until the last few years I ever thought Neal Schusterman's *Unwind* could ever become reality.

Society can't agree on whether it's okay to kill children in utero. How could they ever unite behind the idea that it's okay to kill teenagers and scrape them for parts? Well, I'll tell you.

THE BILL OF LIFE: A HORRIFIC COMPROMISE

As the first book of the series begins, we're told that The Heartland War erupted as an extreme escalation of the abortion debate. It was an actual armed conflict between pro-life and pro-choice factions that tore the country apart. The war's devastating toll created desperate pressure for any resolution that could end the bloodshed. The government's "solution" was the Bill of Life, which retroactively made both sides feel they had "won":

- **For pro-life advocates:** Life became 100% protected from conception to age 13. No

termination of any kind was permitted during
this period.

- **For pro-choice advocates:** Parents gained the
  right to "retroactively abort" their children
  between ages 13-18 through unwinding.

The twisted logic was that unwinding didn't techni-
cally "kill" anyone, since every part of the unwound teen
would live on in different body part recipients.

WHY TEENAGERS SPECIFICALLY?

The funny thing about the Unwind accords is that the
propaganda campaign to dehumanize teens began long
before the bill was signed. The government weaponized
public fear by creating a narrative about "feral" teens –
displaced youth who had supposedly become wild and
dangerous after a civil war. These teens, many of whom
were simply trying to survive, were portrayed as inherently threatening. Their normal behaviors were reframed
as pathological, their very existence presented as a danger
to civilized society.

The government and media essentially weaponized
public fear of these displaced youth by:

- Portraying groups of unsupervised teens as
  inherently dangerous
- Amplifying incidents of theft, vandalism, or
  other survival-driven behaviors
- Framing normal teenage rebellion as
  pathological when it occurred in "unwanted"
  kids

Then, after the cannibalizing began, when older people got new hearts, new hands, new eyes, just because they liked the color better, suddenly there was an expanding of the definition of "feral youth." What started as concern about truly abandoned children gradually expanded to include any teen whose behavior parents found unmanageable:

- Learning disabilities, mental health issues, or simply strong-willed personalities became grounds for unwinding consideration.
- The bar for what constituted a "problem child" kept lowering.

On a societal level, no one paid much mind. Why would they? The young had already been stripped of their humanity. Instead, they were only an entry on a balance sheet: are you a benefit to my (the parent's) life? Or would you be more useful as spare parts?

They had been given their moral "get out of jail free" card. You're not actually ending a life. You are allowing this person, who has wasted the life he or she was given, to continue living though someone else.

The kids themselves are told, "You want to be useful, don't you? We gave you the opportunity to live well. But you didn't. Those bits and bobs of usefulness you have will go to someone with more drive. It's not fair to deprive them when they have the potential that you didn't take advantage of."

It's communism times ten with a religious veneer. You have something I want. And I'm going to convince everyone that it is righteous for me to steal it by force.

THE "FERAL YOUTH" PROPAGANDA MACHINE IS ALREADY RUNNING

In Shusterman's dystopian world, the government weaponized public fear by creating a narrative about "feral" teens in the aftermath of war. But we don't need a civil war to create our feral youth narrative. We have algorithms.

Every platform is force-feeding you the most extreme examples of young male dysfunction. The algorithm doesn't show you the millions of young men working, studying, volunteering, or living normal lives. It shows you Jack Doherty, a 21-year-old sociopath who has built a multi-million-dollar empire by livestreaming his complete disregard for human life. It shows you an endless parade of TikTok "pranksters" destroying property, harassing strangers, and terrorizing communities.

And just like in Shusterman's world, we're not examining the systemic failures that created these conditions. We're not asking why these young men are so desperate for attention that they'll risk their lives and freedom for viral moments. We're not addressing the economic hopelessness, the elimination of stable career paths, the housing crisis that makes independence impossible, or the complete absence of meaningful mentorship and community that has left an entire generation of young men rootless and angry. To say nothing of the way young men and women of child-bearing age have been pitted against each other as enemies.

Instead, we're pathologizing them, viewing them as a threat to the very civilization they're supposed to be inheriting. We're calling them weak, entitled, dangerous. We're creating the exact same psychological conditions that made unwinding seem reasonable in Shusterman's fictional society.

The headlines are already writing themselves: "Young Men Are Falling Behind." "Male Violence on the Rise." "Generation Z Can't Handle Reality." Sound familiar? This is how societies prepare themselves to view certain groups as expendable.

THE CANNIBALIZATION OF YOUTH FOR THE BENEFIT OF AGE

Here's where things get absolutely fucking disgusting. We don't need to wait for some future dystopian legislation to see older generations literally consuming younger ones. **It's happening right now.**

In the Unwind universe, unwinding was never just about getting rid of "problem" teens, but harvesting their healthy young bodies to benefit older, wealthier recipients.

The economic parallels to our current system are impossible to ignore. We live in a society where older generations have structured the economy to extract wealth from younger generations while offering them fewer opportunities for advancement.

Young people work in the gig economy without benefits while their labor enriches older shareholders. They pay into Social Security systems that may not exist when they reach retirement age. They're charged exorbitant amounts for education and healthcare while older Americans benefited from subsidized college and employer-provided health insurance.

In essence, we already have a system where older Americans consume the economic vitality of younger Americans while justifying it as "how the system works" and "paying your dues." The leap to literally consuming their physical vitality while using the same justifications isn't as large as we'd like to believe.

YOU ARE BEING PROGRAMMED

None of this is happening by accident. That constant stream of "young people behaving badly" content flooding your feeds? **It's not random.** It's algorithmic manipulation designed to manufacture your consent for viewing young people as problems to be solved rather than humans to be supported.

When you see video after video of young men acting destructively, ask yourself these questions:

- **Why am I being shown this content?**
- **Who profits from my rage toward young people?**
- **What am I being conditioned to accept?**

The answer should terrify you. A society that views its young people as inherently problematic is a society that's more likely to accept harsh measures to control them. Every viral video of Jack Doherty being a psychopath makes it easier to justify expanded surveillance on all young men. Every clip of Neon threatening children makes it easier to pass legislation restricting young people's rights. Every TikTok prank gone wrong makes it easier to blame individual young people for systemic failures rather than addressing the underlying causes.

You are being programmed to see young people as disposable.

The tech companies and media organizations profiting

from this rage-inducing content aren't necessarily trying to create conditions for dystopian legislation. But they are creating the psychological conditions that make such legislation more palatable.

When we're constantly exposed to the worst examples of youth behavior, we become numb to their humanity. We start seeing them as statistics, threats to be managed, rather than people who need help. This is exactly the mindset necessary for a society to accept something as horrific as unwinding.

No one wants to die, but the fear of death and delusion that you can live forever by refusing to step aside is destroying the greatest civilization to ever exist.

It doesn't work that way.

And if you wish it did... then I encourage to sit with that for a moment. And ask yourself if you're really the good guy in this scenario.

CHAPTER 17
THE OLD MAN YOU DIDN'T KNOW YOU NEEDED

BATTLESHIP (2012) IS HARDLY cinematic gold. But I love it for one reason. Or should I say one <u>scene</u>.

After alien ships demolish young Lt. Hopper's ship, and all the other ships in the area, he needs a new one. But all there is left is an old one. Specifically the USS Missouri. The problem is that none of these young sailors know how to operate this floating antique.

Lucky for them, the Missouri is a museum. One staffed by veterans who DO know how to operate it.

Alex Hopper: You men have given so much to your country, and no one has the right to ask any more of you... but I'm asking.

Old Salt: What do you need, son?

The old WW2 and Vietnam vets then proceed to help the youngins whip some alien ass.

They can't figure out the debit card machine at the grocery store. But they sure as hell remember how to operate the ship they cut their teeth on forty or fifty years ago.

It's glorious.

I started thinking about this thanks to copywriter extraordinaire <u>Nabeel Azeez</u>. In his newsletter, he pointed to the gender dynamics of women in male-dominated fields. In fiction and in real life, these women excelled because an older man took the woman with promise under his wing:

Midge (Mrs. Maisel) owes her career to Lenny Bruce (one of the pioneers of stand-up comedy as it's performed today.)

In season one, Midge gets blackballed right as she's getting started and can't book gigs anywhere in New York.

During a set, Lenny invites Midge on stage to do a short set before he does his own.

He sees something in her and his endorsement lifts the ban and starts her career for real.

Her innate talent then allows her to rocket past other comedians in success and stardom.

Something similar happens between Peggy Olson and Freddy Rumsen, and then Don Draper in Mad Men.

Freddy "discovers" Peggy has an innate talent for copywriting and mentions it to Don.

Don, as creative director and a copywriter himself, is astute enough to give her a shot and mentors her until she becomes a Copy Chief and manages her own team.

Behind every strong independent wahmen is a man who gave her her shot, or one who pushes her to achieve her potential.

As a former female Marine, it struck a cord. I was lucky enough to have an older man **and** an older woman team up to act as my second set of parents in my first duty station, kicking my ass in gear and teaching me how to be a professional.

Boomers, both of them. Both from hard-scrabble, working-class backgrounds. Both rose to excellence because they had mentors of their own. They both went on to be high-ranking Pentagon officials after they turned in their uniforms.

They are the ones who looked at my work and said: "Not good enough. Do it again." They said it over and over again until I did it right the first time.

THE MENTORSHIP GAP

As the eldest of Millennials (b. 1981) and seeing the crop of kids coming up behind me, I have to wonder... who will we ask for help when the Boomers are gone?

Are we in a position to guide the next crop of adults?

Millennials take a lot of guff for the fact that our younger members use the verb "adulting" like it's an accomplishment. But for all our flaws, we are the last generation to have been raised without social media, constant access to the internet, and being filmed everywhere we went.

It is obvious by now that distinction makes a difference in our development, our capability, and, of course, our attention span.

The online learning economy is booming, and many of the courses out there are far more useful than what you find on university campuses these days.

But I'm worried about actual mentorship vs simple skill acquisition.

In order to listen and apply the tough love of a mentor, the criticism that makes you truly excellent at what you do, you have to respect and care about the person giving it to you.

If someone yells at you, "This is crap! You're better

than this; you're just being lazy!" In order to take that critique to heart, the person has to matter to you.

- You must care about their opinion.
- You must want to live the type of life they live
- You must believe they want the best for you

If those elements are not present, then any sharply-worded statement, no matter how true, will be discarded.

That's why anonymous commenters on Twitter get told to pound sand. I don't know you, I don't like you, and I don't care what you think. Kindly piss off.

Unfortunately, for young people today, "Twitter friends" might be the deepest level of relationship they ever form, which is bad news for all of us.

True excellence *always* requires struggle, and taking heat from someone who knows better than you. A coach, a boss, a teacher.

Unfortunately, the overarching mantra for Zoomers seems to be, "It ain't that deep, bro."

But it is.

Whether you're an engineer or a music composer (do those even exist anymore?) we as a society need those truly great talents to come along and change the paradigm every once in a while.

Without the guiding hand of a mentor, a trusted teacher who you obey when he says "Put down the TikTok and get back to work," we will be left with a world of bland mediocrity, one that will have long-lasting implications.

Fifty years from now, when the Zoomers are old and the next generation calls on them for help from the olden times, will they have any help to give?

I'm not sure. But if they are to have a shot at rising to the potential within them, it must be the Millennials who help them reach it.

The Boomers have done their duty.

I think it's time we stepped up.

CHAPTER 18
THE OLD WOMAN YOU DIDN'T KNOW YOU NEEDED

MAD MAX: *Fury Road* was an objectively good movie, and one of the best times I've ever had in the theater. The story, the acting, the sheer audacity of it... all wonderful.

The movie was also remarkable in that it gave us something we don't often see (then or now): Middle-aged and old women, a whole group of them being portrayed positively AND realistically.

There's no shortage of perfect girl bosses in film and TV. Collectively, we're all rather sick of them. The Many Mothers—bad asses though they were—were not given super powers. They were women, with all the frailty that implies, though they powered through those frailties to make a difference. They identified themselves, first and foremost, as mothers. As caregivers. As people who make things grow. And in their brief time with the young women under their care, they were able to pass on that wisdom and steer the girls away from cynicism.

Even in the most wholesome of Hallmark movies, we don't get a lot of this from older women on the screen.

Instead, we are more often confronted with meddling

mothers and mothers-in-law, conniving women like Gemma Teller from *Sons of Anarchy*, who are hellbent on ruining the joy of younger women.

Bitterness is a common theme in older women (We all remember the mom from *Titanic*). Worse, we're now being confronted with a slew of "cougars," who behave like desperate, oversexed predators, all while complaining about similar behavior when displayed by men.

If you have never heard of MILF Island, consider yourself lucky.

WHO ARE YOUNG WOMEN SUPPOSED TO LOOK UP TO?

These pervasive archetypes seem to set up a weird combativeness between older women and younger women. Like we're competing.

A male character is often seen as a mentor to both sexes. It works and it's realistic. Females generally do not mentor males—at work or in their personal lives. Only in very rare cases. Get mad if you want. Point to the one case in a million. It's cool.

But as a rule, it doesn't happen. And if you think it does, ask yourself, is it the young man pointing to the older woman, saying "Yep, she's my mentor." Or is it the woman taking that title for herself?

Women mentor other women. Or at least they used to.

TV has been better at this than movies, at least in my own limited experience. If any true cinephiles out there disagree, feel free to let me know.

Sheldon's Mom on *The Big Bang Theory* is an excellent example. A loving southern woman who cares for her unusual son and takes the time to help mentor Penny, her son's neighbor. She visits only occasionally, but her warmth shines through her sternness to the point that even young, liberal Penny doesn't get defensive when Sheldon's mom advises her to wear less slutty tops on a first date to communicate she's looking for something serious.

Going back farther, Marilla Cuthbert from *Anne of Green Gables* has to be the pinnacle of female mentorship. Far from the badass heroines of *Mad Max: Fury Road*, Marilla is an old maid who lives with her brother. She and her brother adopt an orphan, wanting a boy to help with manual labor around the farm. Instead, they get the ginger tornado, Anne Shirley.

Anne is in need of some mentorship. How to hold her temper. How to apologize. How to be a regal lady even with limited means.

Marilla is stern and won't put up with any nonsense. But she's not hard and she's not mean, which is rare in TV these days.

Often when a female character says something like "I don't take any shit," what she truly means is that she is an awful person and is pleased by that.

LETTING WOMEN GROW UP

While TV has done right by older women, it can commit the sin of keeping their women characters in a perpetual state of 20-something immaturity. Comedies in particular are bad about this. Think of *Friends*.

Yeah, they entered relationships and had kids. But look at their behavior. Did they grow up? Did Monica or Rachel really mature in the ten years the show was on the air?

Or *Gilmore Girls*. That was even more egregious. The show ran for seven seasons, but came back with a mini-series thirteen years after the fact. Lorelei, the mother, was just as childish and silly as she had been on season 1 of the show and Rory, the daughter, was WORSE. So much worse!

I will give the show props for its treatment of Emily, Lorelei's mother. Though insufferable and snooty, her arc was the most satisfying in my opinion.

This broad-scale infantilism wasn't done as a plot point. I suspect it was unintentional. The writers just kept them this way and I think it has a lot to do with our collective fear of acting OLD.

I previously wrote about how the word "Matronly" has become a slur, though it didn't use to be. Instead, we now have the expectation for women in their 50s to adopt the same look, lifestyle, and mannerisms as girls in their 20s. Why? Is that progress?

TEENS LISTEN TO MEDIA MORE THAN REAL PEOPLE. DEAL WITH IT.

Rather than complain about the fact that young women will listen to other idiot Zoomers on TikTok while ignoring their mother's sage advice, I'd like to make fictionalized woman mentors more available to them.

TV in general needs to improve in our current entertainment season, but the representation of older women as mentors is especially in need of attention.

Older women sharing their hard-won experience protects younger, more vulnerable women. Not only from predatory men, though that's a big part of it.

They also serve to protect younger women from our accommodating nature. And it IS our nature to be agreeable. Don't let anyone tell you society made us this way.

There's a reason women with autism don't fit in with girl groups. The natural agreeableness and consensus-seeking found in females is diminished or entirely absent in girls with autism. They see the pervasiveness of this quality among women because they themselves lack it.

Average young women don't see it because a fish does not perceive the water in which it swims.

Older women, especially those well past dating and childrearing, are the ones who can point out what girls cannot yet perceive. Ideally it would be a real-life woman to do this. But not every girl is so lucky.

Let there be more Marillas in film and TV. Let a girl see what it looks like to have an older woman be badass in ways that have nothing to do with throwing a grenade or saying mean things without provocation.

And not to be selfish about it, but as I reach a certain age... maybe I'd like someone to look up to as well.

PART SIX
THE THREATS WITHOUT AND WITHIN

CHAPTER 19
IT'S WHAT'S INSIDE:
THE RAGE OF
COWARDS

"IF THE GRASS *is greener on the other side, maybe you should water your own lawn." - Ghandi, probably*

There are few things in life as repulsive as self-pity, a person crying about their circumstances while doing nothing to change them.

For some people, the self-pity has moved beyond their circumstances and has encompassed their whole being: they no longer hate their life; they hate themselves.

And the strange part about it is that many of these people are just out living their lives. Far from being curled in a ball of cookie-dough-eating depression, they're seeing movies, chatting with friends, and going to work.

But make no mistake, they hate themselves. And they'd do anything to be someone else.

It's cool to dump on the state of modern movie making, but I'm happy to say there are some bangers out there, and last year's It's What's Inside is one of them.

The movie asked us to consider, "What if you didn't *have* to be yourself? What if you could be someone else?"

The premise of the movie is that a group of friends get together for a party, only to find that an unexpected guest arrives with a machine that can put your consciousness into someone else's body.

And you stay in that other person's body until you activate the same machine again, undoing the switcheroo.

If you watch the trailer, you can see it's a pretty big group of friends, and they vary in their levels of self-esteem and esteem for others. And boy, can you see the difference when they get a taste of being in someone else's skin.

I generally spoil movies in my articles, but for this one, I'll keep the spoilers to a minimum. I liked it a lot, and I think you probably will too, so I don't want to take the punch out of the ending.

A SHITTY LIFE YOU KEEP CHOOSING

It's an ensemble cast, but the primary focus of the film is on Shelby, an insecure 20-something who is fundamentally shaped by jealousy , specifically for her friend, Nikki, who is a massive social media influencer.

Nikki is also "the one who got away" for Cyrus... Shelby's current boyfriend.

Given what an absolute shit bag Cyrus is, it's easy to feel sorry for Shelby—to view her as the victim. But as we find out, she has stayed with him for NINE years. Nine years of no ring. Nine years of him preferring to masturbate than have sex with her.

And this isn't a frigid girlfriend situation either.

The first time we even see Shelby, she's wearing a red lingerie and blonde wig (mimicking Nikki's mannerisms) and is excited to start a sexual role-play with her boyfriend. She wants to entice him so he won't need the porn.

Except when she walks into the bedroom in her wig and lingerie, she finds Cyrus masturbating. She can't see the screen on the laptop, but we can.

He's cranking it to Nikki.

The film invites us to feel bad for her... and we do. It's hard not to. She's a timid, passive person, a quality many men actually seek out in a girl. Cyrus, on the other hand, criticizes and mocks her for it.

And Shelby is aware she's being mistreated. Later on, she laments that Cyrus spent years of gaslighting making her insecure about her own body. This undermining of Shelby's self-confidence resulted in her becoming increasingly dependent on Cyrus's validation while simultaneously making her feel inadequate.

It's plain he doesn't actually like her. He never did, and we don't need to wait for the script to spell it out for us. It's obvious in the first five minutes.

But still she stays. Even as she knows he never actually wanted her.

It's the sick relationship dynamic that she has chosen, telling herself she has no power to change it.

BEING A VICTIM DOESN'T MEAN YOU'RE GOOD

The funny thing is that Shelby never wanted to participate in the body-swap game. She only did it because Cyrus pressured her into it. But wouldn't you know, Shelby ends up in Nikki's body during the second round of the body-swap game, and only then does it occur to her that she has power over what she does.

Part of the reason she put up with Cyrus's crap is because she idealized her friend's life to the point of obsession: "I am not Nikki, therefore I am not good, therefore I deserve to be mistreated." It's gross, obviously, but there's a social media aspect to all this that hits the mark for Zoomers and younger millennials.

But spending time in Nikki's body, and everything that happens afterward, doesn't change who Shelby is—it reveals who she always was.

Her "liberation" from Cyrus at the end of the movie is controversial as hell, and for good reason. Yes, she breaks free from her former passivity... but in a way that is far outsized to what Cyrus deserves.

Especially since she could have left at any time!

Cyrus was an asshole, a sneering, condescending prick who settled for a girl he didn't like because the one he actually wanted didn't want him back. That's mean and it's sad. But the list of grievances Shelby had to justify her actions only existed because of her own choices.

Her act of betrayal represents both her revenge and her liberation from a relationship built on lies and manipulation. And some (a lot?) of the girlies cheered at what she did.

I guess that's an easy reaction to have. Better that than to reflect on the reality that all those boys who treated you like Cyrus treated Shelby only did so because you let them. It's easier to laugh at a shit head getting an unexpected ending than it is to ask yourself: what unpleasant reality am I accepting in exchange for security/attention/lust?

It would be even more difficult to ask yourself: What would happen if I just stopped? What if I just walked away from this bullshit and did something else?

But maybe you should. If you don't, you may wake up one day and realize that you have become Shelby. And I mean that in the worst possible way.

CHAPTER 20
INVINCIBLE: ADDICTIVE RAGE

"ANGER, *if not restrained, is frequently more hurtful to us than the injury that provokes it.*" - *Lucius Annaeus Seneca*

There's a funny idea about anger that if you just "let it out," you'll be free of its hold over you and can move on, returning to your presumed state of calm and kindness once you let off some steam.

Unfortunately, that isn't always—or even often—the case.

Season 3 of Invincible (Prime original) wrapped yesterday, and we saw our main super-powered character, Mark, make a fateful decision.

Sometimes people just need to die, and he's okay with being the one to make that happen.

It was a full circle moment, as at the end of season 2, Mark had a psychological break over killing Angstrom Levy—a nasty piece of work who severely injured his mom and infant brother and nearly got Mark killed.

After seeing his mother's arm snapped off in a completely unprovoked assault, Mark pummeled Angstrom to death, smashing his skull into pulp.

"I thought he was stronger! He said he was stronger now."

Mark is 19, and the son of a murderous alien who killed thousands of people in Season 1.

In his desperation to not be like his father, Mark is inconsolable at having killed a guy who very much deserved it and would have been a continuing threat had he been allowed to live. His hangups with not being like his dad are a problem; even at his young age, he knows perfectly well that prison is no obstacle for some villains. Yet he clings to the childish idea that he should never kill anyone ever.

Until he doesn't.

ANGER AS ADDICTION: THE DANGEROUS SPIRAL

In the early episodes of Season 3, Mark's anger starts to get the better of him, as does his sense of moral right-eousness.

He's stronger than almost everyone else, therefore he has a duty to protect them, right? And because he's one of the good guys, then he gets to decide who the bad guys are, right?

In his crash-out over his dad and his sort-of-accidental killing of Angstrom Levy, Mark starts giving into the nasty side of being the strongest guy in the room.

It gets so bad that he lashes out at Cecil, director of the Global Defense Agency and sort of an uncle figure in Mark's life. In dealing with his anger, Mark lashes out at Cecil, seemingly thinking of him as a safe target.

But Cecil isn't one to let that kind of thing slide and he confronts Mark about his aggressive behavior.

Cecil: "You see things one way and you won't make room for any other viewpoint. You threaten people who disagree with you."

Mark: "I don't threaten!"

Cecil: "No? Because you're scaring the shit out of me right now."

Hearing Cecil say that is terrifying in itself. This man doesn't blink and has been presiding over super-powered, super-strong beings for most of his adult life.

Unfortunately, it's not enough to shake Mark out of his rage spiral, and there are some severe consequences for that.

Mark's struggle with guilt and escalating rage mirrors real-world patterns of anger addiction (as well as the unchecked emotions of teenagers).

Far from the "letting off steam" analogy, giving into anger actually makes it stronger within us.

To be clear, anger is an important survival mechanism. It triggers our fight-or-flight response, preparing us to confront threats. The amygdala activates, adrenaline and cortisol flood our system, and our bodies prepare for action. This response served our ancestors well when facing predators or rival tribes.

And it serves us well today when car trouble finds us in the wrong neighborhood at night.

For Mark, his anger initially serves a protective function—defending his family against genuine threats. However, as the show portrays, the line between protective anger and destructive rage can blur quickly.

That's because the neurochemical cocktail that activates anger can become addictive.

Getting pissed off triggers dopamine release, creating a neurochemical reward that can reinforce angry behavior. A 2019 study showed that people who frequently express anger experience this dopamine "high" more intensely than others.

It starts off as a crutch, an emotional self-medication. That temporary feeling of power and control masks the underlying feelings of vulnerability or fear. But the thing is, <u>studies have shown</u> giving into regular anger episodes creates neural pathways that make future anger responses more likely and more intense—similar to addiction pathways.

And just like any addict, the rageaholics find a lot of ways to justify their addiction.

THE SELECTIVE NATURE OF "UNCONTROLLABLE" ANGER

If you've ever dealt with someone with anger issues, or if you were a viewer of Dr. Phil, then Mark's choice to lash out at Cecil (a person without powers) might have been familiar to you. It's curious, isn't it, how supposedly "uncontrollable" anger frequently appears only against specific people or in specific contexts?

Like against weaker people or in the privacy of their home.

Dr. Lundy Bancroft, in his extensive work with abusive individuals, documented a pattern he calls "selective explosive disorder"—a twist on the clinical diagnosis of intermittent explosive disorder. His research with thousands of anger management clients revealed that many people who claim they "just lose control" actually demonstrate remarkable selectivity in where and with whom they "lose control."

Consider these patterns: workplace bullies who exhibit explosive anger at subordinates but somehow never with superiors or clients. Or the concept of "upscale abuse" where high-functioning individuals maintain perfect composure in professional and social settings while exhibiting terrifying rage at home.

These people never "lost control" in contexts that might damage their reputation or career.

Funny that.

BREAKING THE CYCLE

In bringing Season 3 to a close, Mark gets a grip on his anger because of the same stimulus that caused him to lose it in the first place: love for his family and girlfriend.

Seeing Angstrom Levy had survived what should have been a fatal blow and all of the thousands of deaths that came from Levy's second attack, Mark understood that anger should be listened to sometimes, specifically to protect yourself and those you care about.

But keep it aimed where it belongs and wrestle it back in the cage when you're done with it.

Don't wait until it's done with you.

CHAPTER 21

DARKNESS FEEDS ON WEAKNESS

IN OUR THERAPY-SATURATED CULTURE, we're constantly told to "heal in your own time" and "accept yourself as you are." It sounds compassionate, affirming. When in actuality, it's the best way to make yourself easy prey.

Horror movies have an uncomfortable way of revealing truths we'd rather ignore. Strip away the supernatural elements, the gore, and the jump scares, and you'll find something far more terrifying: evil doesn't create weakness. It simply waits for the right moment to exploit what's already there.

Stress and guilt are emotions we all struggle with. But if they're left to fester, it may just be that everyone we love will suffer for it.

SESSION 9: STRESS WILL TAKE YOUR SOUL

Session 9 (2001) makes a lot of movie reviewers top ten lists, and for good reasons. Filmed on location in a real dilapidated mental asylum, the audience is left feeling dread from beginning to end, with the final line living rent free in every viewer's head for years to come:

I live in the weak and the wounded.

Gordon Fleming is one of our main characters—a decent enough guy. He's a hard-working asbestos removal contractor, trying to provide for his wife and new baby (which is dealing with colic and crying ceaselessly). He's also in a fair bit of financial distress, something made clear in the first scene of the movie s he agrees to a preposterous deadline to clear the asbestos in the asylum. His team doesn't like it, but they all rally to put in the long days to get the job done. They know Gordon needs the money. Badly.

It doesn't take long for Gordon's behavior to deteriorate. Just being in the asylum makes everyone on edge, especially since there's so many objects and memories left behind by both the patients and the staff. Gordon becomes increasingly erratic, snapping at his crew, making dangerous decisions, and keeps reflecting back on a terrible fight he had with his wife the night before the job started.

All the while, another member of the crew, Mike, finds tapes of old therapy sessions with a patient named Mary— a woman with multiple personalities. Supposedly. The recordings themselves become a kind of mirror. The therapist's voice describing a patient who is "weak and disturbed" could just as easily be describing Gordon's current state.

It becomes apparent through those therapy tapes that there's something more than memories in the asylum. And that thing got its claws into Gordon.

What makes Gordon uniquely vulnerable was that unlike his crew members, who treated their problems as external challenges to be managed, Gordon internalized his failures.

He doesn't just have financial problems; he *is* a financial failure. He doesn't just have a sick baby and an overwhelmed wife; he's a father who can't provide peace for his family. This internalization creates the perfect conditions for "Simon" to work from the inside out.

The shocking reveal that Gordon has been systematically murdering his crew members isn't really shocking if you've been paying attention to his psychological trajectory. A man who has already decided he's a failure is a man primed to become something monstrous. Simon only provided the final justification for someone who was already collapsing under the weight of his own self-recrimination.

"Do it, Gordon."

Unaddressed stress and trauma metastasize. They create vulnerabilities that patient predators—whether supernatural or human—will eventually exploit. Gordon's descent into violence was the logical endpoint of a man who chose to manage his problems rather than solve them, and who had already begun to see himself as the problem that needed to be solved.

EVENT HORIZON: WHEN GUILT BECOMES YOUR GHOST

At first blush, 1997's *Event Horizon* could have passed for a hard scifi movie. The movie begins with a rescue mission to retrieve the lost starship Event Horizon. Dr. Weir, the ship's creator, joins Captain Miller's crew to investigate what happened when the ship's experimental gravity drive malfunctioned and the ship vanished for seven years. What they find is a vessel that has been to hell—literally—and brought something back with it.

Almost immediately the ship begins tormenting each crew member with personalized nightmares drawn from their darkest memories and deepest guilts. One by one, they're driven to madness, suicide, and murder.

Dr. Weir carries the crushing guilt of his wife Claire's suicide—a death that occurred while he was obsessing over his work instead of attending to their deteriorating relationship.

Captain Miller carries his own trauma from a fire on the ship Goliath where he was forced to leave crew members behind to save the rest. The Event Horizon shows him those burning men too, tries to break him with visions of their deaths.

But unlike Weir, who accepts the condemnation from the ghostly visage of Claire, Miller recognizes these visions as attacks, as lies designed to weaken him. His guilt hasn't consumed his identity the way Weir's has.

By the climax, Weir has become indistinguishable from the malevolent force he originally wanted to study. Miller dies fighting to save others; Weir dies trying to damn them. The difference isn't in their circumstances or their trauma—it's that Miller carried his burden, and Weir let his burden carry him.

GROWTH IS YOUR ARMOR

The real horror is the realization that we're all carrying around potential weapons that could be used against us. Every unresolved issue, every character defect we've decided to live with, every area where we've chosen comfort over growth represents a possible entry point for something that doesn't have our best interests at heart.

That's why Catholic priests who perform exorcisms have to go to confession and receive the Eucharist before confronting the demon.

The protagonists in these films all had opportunities to address their weaknesses. They had warning signs, concerned friends, and moments of clarity where they could have chosen differently. But they consistently chose short-term comfort over long-term safety. They prioritized avoiding difficult conversations over having them. They selected familiar dysfunction over unfamiliar growth.

Every one of these choices made them more vulnerable to the forces that eventually destroyed them.

This is how real predators work too.

Abusers don't target the strongest, most self-aware people. They target those with unresolved trauma, boundary issues, and desperate needs they haven't learned to meet in healthy ways. Cult leaders don't convert happy, fulfilled individuals—they recruit people who are searching for meaning, belonging, and purpose they haven't found elsewhere.

The horror movie monsters are metaphors, but the psychological patterns they exploit are real. Every weakness we leave unaddressed, every trauma we decide to "manage" rather than heal, every character defect we choose to accept rather than overcome—these become potential weapons in the hands of anyone smart enough and patient enough to use them against us.

Your demons are patient. They'll wait for just the right moment to strike.

The question is: will you give it to them?

CHAPTER 22
YOUR NIGHTMARES ARE REAL

ON A RECENT APPEARANCE on the <u>Dad Lit Podcast</u>, I was asked why I wrote paranormal—what about it appealed to me. My answer was simple.

Our legends, myths, and supernatural entities are real and pretending they're not is a mistake. Demons walk among us and they're right there for all to see.

To be clear, I don't think all supernatural creatures are real. At least not anymore. We can be fairly certain the giants are gone, for instance. But I won't be convinced they weren't around in times past.

I'm 50/50 on vampires, honestly. But I think if they ever did exist, they were of the hideous Count Orlock (Nosferatu) variety rather than sexy-goodtime Erik Northman (True Blood) flavor.

I bring it up because I just got done watching <u>Weapons</u>, which is in "holy-shit-it's-good" territory. I have so much to say but don't want to spoil it for you, so I thought I would skip the movie tie-in and go straight to the life advice.

Besides, you've heard this all from me before.

There's a point in *Weapons* where the cause of all the horror is revealed. Neither the audience, nor the characters on screen know precisely what they're dealing with yet. But they know the creature in the doorway is bad. It doesn't belong there, and it is asking to be let into their house.

In this case, I'm not sure declining the invitation would have saved all the characters in question, but maybe one of them would have gotten out alive at least.

Which brings me to my first lesson: Listen to your gut.

I won't go on a persuasive diatribe on why you MUST believe in the paranormal or supernatural. You don't have to. But whether you believe or not, you know when you encounter someone who is *wrong*. They don't move right. They don't talk right. They're wrong—you just can't put your finger on exactly why.

May I remind you that <u>uncanny valley</u> is an inborn instinct in all humans. Take a moment and ask yourself why.

It's not a good idea to push away what your instincts are screaming at you because you think you're being silly.

It might be the last mistake you ever make.

This year's other surprise success *Sinners*, also demonstrated the importance of listening to your gut and being versed on your lore. Annie, our boobalicious queen, found it highly suspicious that one of her friends suddenly couldn't enter the premises without an invitation. And she didn't push it away.

Like I said, I'm 50-50 on the vampires. But I know there's a lot of monsters who rely on your refusal to be impolite, to sit in discomfort. They relish the fact that you'll accommodate the creature right up until it kills you.

Lesson Two: Your gut trumps manners

Few lines have stuck with me as violently as the last lines of Speak No Evil:

Bjorn: Why are you doing this?
Patrick: Because you let me.

The article I wrote about it leaned into the gender dynamics because that was one of the big changes in the American version vs the original Danish film. But the rule applies to everyone. Those who want to victimize you will often take the time to make you feel bad for not making it easy for them.

"Oh, are you scurred because I'm a man/black/poor?"

"Why are you being rude when all I want to do is come in and get a drink of water?"

Let your instincts feel no shame.

And it's not just scummy people who set off your danger signals. It's easier to listen when the person looks outlandish. A lot easier. The final rule is, for obvious reasons, the hardest for most people to take to heart and apply in their own life.

Rule Three: Be no respecter of persons.

"You guys, I'm so excited! Puff Daddy, the filthy rich, mega powerful music producer wants a meeting with me! Isn't that great? I mean, yeah, it's at his gated house. And I'm not allowed to bring my mom. And no one else is going to be there. And I had to sign an NDA that promised horrible consequences if I speak out of turn. But it'll be fine. Right?"

The worst of the demons take pains to put themselves in positions of power before they start preying on people in earnest. They start small of course. Junkies, ex-cons. Assorted ruffians who wouldn't be believed even if they bothered to report what happened. But once they have power and respectability, that's when the horns come out.

And yes, that goes for the church too.

No one likes the idea of having to always be on your guard, to never trust anyone ever. But really, you don't have to. You just have to stick to what you know is true.

Business deals sometimes happen in hotel rooms, but not one-on-one, and not in a fucking bathrobe.

Ask yourself why you're being asked to keep a secret? Why are you being steered away from the crowd? Why are you being told that every rule and standard you've learned in life is "just not the way it's done here?"

You don't have to jump at shadows and feel you're about to be attacked at any moment. You only have to look at people's actions, the circumstances surrounding them, and cross-reference to what you know is correct and normal behavior. When it's off, you know it.

All you have to do is listen.

There are sometimes good reasons to willingly walk into danger. But being afraid of offending the monster who's come to harm you should never be one of them.

CHAPTER 23
THE SLANDER OF BLACK AMERICANS

THE AMERICAN MOVIE consumer has been screaming at studios for years. No, we DON'T like over-powered, poorly written female characters with no flaws beating up likeable male characters. And no, we don't like our treasured movie franchises being vandalized for the sake of woke ideology.

Luckily, the studios have finally listened. We've been consistently voting with our wallets and the lawyers and money men have clearly snapped the whip, bringing the idealogue directors, producers, and actors to heel.

Nice.

But since we're making changes in entertainment, there's another pressing issue that I'd like to fix, if you don't mind.

THE VICIOUS SLANDER OF BLACK AMERICAN CULTURE

Since 2016, mainstream media has taken a nasty turn in its portrayal of Black Americans. Music, film, popular culture. Somehow, every media outlet gave us booty shaking female rappers, criminalized, sexualized black children spewing filth on YouTube, and sub-80 IQ adults proudly proclaiming their past (and current) crimes. And then they called it Black American culture.

No. It isn't. And it never has been.

Before I get too deep into this, I know there are some melanated brethren (and neurotic white people) who will take issue with my pasty ass even daring to talk about this. I don't care.

I do not see you as separate from white Americans. We don't do "blood and soil" here. You are my people and a part of my culture. So I'm not going to apologize for my glow-in-the-dark, red-headed self having an opinion. Those days are over.

Somehow, despite significant Black economic mobility and educational achievement (particularly in women), entertainment platforms have insisted on promoting and glorifying the nasty stereotypes previous generations worked so hard to dispel.

Remember all those Black guys who held signs saying "I am a man?" Remember how Black women fought against the idea that they were just bodies to be sexually degraded?

Millennials decided that was "respectability politics," which was bad. So once they took over the arts, they gave us Ice Spice and a movie literally titled *The Society of Magical Negros* starring a self-loathing mixed-race man. For fuck's sake.

We also got a spate of slavery- and racism-focused suffering porn. Since 2015, the mainstream shift in Black cinema toward *12 Years a Slave, Harriet,* and *The Hate U Give* was obvious and ubiquitous.

Gone was the vibe of 90s and 00s movies like Ice

Cube's *Friday* series, which offered pure comedy. Yes, it featured stereotypes like financial struggles, pot smoking, and gun violence. But it was played for laughs (effectively). It was not painted as aspiration or as the written-in-stone fate of every Black person.

Spike Lee's *Crooklyn* showed us a dramatic and comical portrait of family life in 1970s Brooklyn, while films like *Love Jones* and *Brown Sugar* explored romance among young Black professionals. (Employed AND Black?? Impossible! The white man would never allow it!)

Soul Food celebrated family traditions and intergenerational bonds, while *Love & Basketball* told a story of athletic ambition and a friendship turned romance. These movies all shared Black joy, love, ambition, and *everyday* experiences. Some of them acknowledged, but didn't center, discrimination or simple differences in being Black.

Black American culture is, in many ways, distinct from WASP American culture, but ghetto culture is NOT Black culture.

And I'm not the only one who noticed:

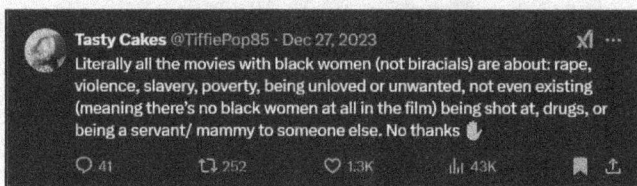

A PROMISING BLACK FUTURE

There have been glimmers of hope. I was blown away by
Netflix's *They Cloned Tyrone*, a scifi comedy centered on
Black people that blended the aesthetic of 70s Blaxploita-
tion, contemporary hip hop, and early 2000s crunk. It was
so funny, the scifi elements were solid, and the performances fantastic.

I will never forgive Disney Star Wars for sidelining
John Boyega. He's amazing.

Likewise, there have been several forays into horror
movies centered on Black people (*Get Out, Deliverance,
Candy Man*) and a return to the Black comedy is looking
promising with the upcoming *One of Them Days* starring
Keke Palmer.

This is what we need, and now that the Covid and
Hollywood strike nonsense is over, it's time to return to
what we had in the 1990s.

We need films that show Black professionals navigating
career challenges, Black families dealing with universal
parent-child dynamics, Black romance in all its complexity,
and Black heroes saving the world—stories where racial
identity informs the character's perspective but doesn't
define their entire narrative.

The Black experience in America is not a monolith, especially considering the ever-increasing number of biracial/mixed people.

Moviegoers deserve to see Black people in every genre —comedy, action, romance, science fiction, and drama— not just in historical pieces or social commentary where we're encouraged to hate and distrust each other.

I don't accept that model of entertainment. I won't praise it, and I won't hold back on my disdain for anyone who has the audacity to declare it as representative of Black American culture.

I ain't having it. And you, my fellow American movie lover of whatever complexion you may be, shouldn't either.

AWESOME BLACK MOVIES

I'm intentionally excluding Tyler Perry movies. No shade, just not for this list. These are Black stories vs movies starring Black People (something like Bad Boys). Django was good too, but we're not doing slavery stories today.

Historical

1. Life
2. Harlem Nights
3. Kingdom Come
4. The Six Triple Eight
5. The Harder They Fall
6. Roll Bounce
7. Black Dynamite
8. Devil in a Blue Dress

Contemporary

1. Barber Shop (all of them)
2. The Wood
3. The Best Man
4. Love and Basketball
5. Waiting to Exhale
6. Soul Food
7. Death at a Funeral (2010)
8. Friday
9. American Fiction
10. The Nutty Professor
11. Boomerang

OTHER (SCIFI/FANTASY)

1. They Cloned Tyrone
2. Blade
3. Vampire in Brooklyn (not great, but I'll allow it)
4. Bones (Also not great, but it could have been)
5. Spawn
6. Candyman (2021)

PART SEVEN
FAMILY, LEGACY, AND REDEMPTION

CHAPTER 24
THE HAUNTING OF HILL HOUSE: FAMILY AND GRIEF

THE HAUNTING *of Hill House* (Netflix) begins on "the last night," when Hugh Crain gathered up his five children in the middle of the night, bundled them in the car, and drove them to a hotel, ignoring their questions about where Mommy was.

Instead of remaining with his children at the hotel, he leaves, telling Steven, the oldest, to take care of his siblings while he goes back for Mommy. When Hugh comes back the following morning, only Nell, the youngest, is awake. She asks her father what is all over his shirt. "Just paint, honey."

As we come to find out, it's not paint at all, and there are some serious questions about what really happened to Mommy and what Hugh knows about it.

Mike Flanagan's limited series captures not only a ghost story, but the underlying horror we all feel at a number of things: dying, mental illness, losing someone we love.

The mystery of Hill House is just the backdrop the

wreckage that has befallen the Crain family since that night in 1992.

No one knows what happened to Olivia Crain, only that she died and her husband was briefly detained by police... but then released. His five children were raised by their mother's sister and all five of them burned with anger. The anger that their father refused to tell anyone what happened in the house that night.

The grief at being robbed of their mother, and even the truth of what happened to her, led to different results. Steven becomes a best-selling author by writing an account of all the strange goings-on in Hill House, including a fictionalized ending of what he "knew" happened... even though he wasn't there and couldn't possibly know.

THE ANGER OF CHILDREN AT THEIR PARENTS IS AN OVERRIDING THEME THROUGHOUT THE SHOW.

We see both sides, not only how justified the children are in their anger at their father, but also how they are angry about the wrong things. And they remember many things wrong. Because they were children.

We often get the idea from movies and tv shows that children are innocent and good, the ultimate arbiters of truth. We must believe the children, so many stories tell us.

The Haunting of Hill House takes a more realistic tack. It is epitomized in a conversation between Hugh and Steven. Hugh tells his son that he read his book, and that many details were wrong.

When Steven scoffs at the idea that he got anything wrong, Hugh snaps back: "We never had a treehouse, Steve. I was working more than 15 hours a day to restore that house, you think I had time to build you a tree fort?"

Steven sat in that treehouse with his brother Luke so many times. How, then, could it be that there was no such place?

For the first time, this sneering holier-than-thou cynic finally realizes that his experiences as a child were not those of perfect understanding. That his father is not the lying screw-up he'd imagined.

Hill House stands as a metaphor for the tricks our human brains play on us to drive a wedge in our relationships: the flawed memories of children, how we are warped by grief, the attempt to control the world around us through a variety of defense mechanisms.

Shirley, the eldest daughter, adapts to the chaos of her mother's death by becoming a control freak so angry at her brother's use of their childhood as literary fodder that she damns her family business into financial straits.

Theodora, the middle child, builds walls so high around herself that not even her family is allowed in.

Luke, the youngest, becomes a good old-fashioned drug addict.

And his twin sister, Nell. My god, how the tragedy of Nell hovers over nearly the entire series. The title speaks of Hill House, but mostly it was Nell who was haunted, both in life and in death. It is she who must suffer visions of her own death, only to spend her afterlife watching her beloved family unravel, helpless to stop them.

It's been months since I binged the show and still I think about it. But why? I am lucky in that I have not suffered through a loved one's premature death. Or a drug-addicted sibling. I have been uncommonly blessed in my life.

Even still, I saw myself in some of the Crain children's defense mechanisms, mostly in Shirley. I too suffer the delusion that if I control myself enough, the world will do my bidding.

But we cannot control what life brings us. We cannot trust our childhood memories of our parents, and the anger we inevitably hold, are the truth. We can only control how we react to what happens to us and how we treat those closest to us.

The Haunting of Hill House is remarkable in that it got the family just right. In all its perfection and imperfection. The show emphatically declares, yes your family matters. No, you cannot replace their love and dedication with casual sex or substance abuse or a group of friends.

Once they are gone, they are gone. So love them while they are here. And tell them you love them while you still can. So few of us get the chance for a parting message. Even fewer have a haunted house of their own, letting you speak to your family long after you're gone.

CHAPTER 25
GILMORE GIRLS: THE BEST DRESSED LOSERS AT THE PARTY

A FEW MONTHS AGO, there was a trending hashtag on Instagram and Facebook #3charactersthatdescribeme. I chose Kira Nirys (*Star Trek: Deep Space Nine*), Barb (*Stranger Things*), and last but not least, Rory Gilmore from *Gilmore Girls*. I based this comparison of myself and Rory on two factors: Who Rory was in the original series (2000-2007) and who I was when I watched her. Years later, things... as they must... have changed.

The strengths of the reboot mini-series are the same as they were in the original series: the charm of Stars Hollow, the relationship between and among Lorelai and Rory and Emily, and the cast of supporting characters. The death of Richard looms large (literally, thanks to a too-big painting in the parlor) and the absence of Edward Herrman is almost its own character.

At least in my life span, Herrman always played wise paternal characters, even when it was all a charade to hide his bloodsucking ways (The Lost Boys). So his death was a genuine sadness in me, which made the funeral scene and

Lorelai's inappropriate storytelling about him all the more real.

Pop culture references abound, including some prolonged schtick about the book/movie Wild and how it inspired flocks of troubled women to go hiking to fix their problems. Because that's how it works, right? The seasonal segmentation of the series works well, because Rory is an adult now; in adulthood, life seems to come more in chunks than in episodes.

The low point in the show was the all-too-real fate of Rory. She with her filthy rich grandparents and her Ivy League education. Despite every benefit, she is drifting, lost in her quest to be a writer, and not just any writer. A famous, New York, glitterati type of writer. It's not going well for her, despite a well-received piece in *The New Yorker*.

Rory is that college friend we all have. The really promising one you meet up for lunch with in your thirties and come away muttering under your breath, "Dude, get your shit together."

But beyond the general highs and lows of the story-telling, I found three overarching themes in the mini-series that, regardless of all else, made the endeavor well worth it.

A LOVE NOTE TO COMMITMENT

Emily is hardly tactful when it comes to her opinions on how life should be, not just for herself, but for Lorelai and pretty much everyone else in the world. But she did have one thing right. She pointed out the foolish cowardice of Lorelai's "partnership" with Luke, the one in which she lived with him and loved him, but made no effort to truly bind their lives together, and certainly no commitment to him.

Perhaps some may have bristled when Emily called Luke and Lorelai roommates, but she was right on the money. Emily focused on their not being married, but the lack of a ring was not the problem—Lorelai dictating the terms was. If you want me, she seems to have said, then you will stay at the distance I put you and never push for more.

In keeping that control, Lorelai thought she was getting what she wanted and what she needed. Because she didn't want to be like her parents. Or perhaps she thought she could never have the bond her parents had. You can see why it would be intimidating—comparing your series of boyfriends to a fifty-year marriage. But in examining her choices, and (I think) really seeing Luke for the first time, she saw that committing to him, for real this time, was what she wanted and needed to do. It was her path to happiness and security.

Our society preaches the gospel of freedom and no attachments from every pulpit. It was nice to see the strength of coupledom taking center stage in Stars Hollow.

An affirmation that our circumstances alone do not dictate our lives

When you look at how Rory's life is, well into her thirties, you would think she came from struggling circumstances. But no. Her fabulously wealthy grandparents paid for her to go to the aforementioned prestigious prep school. Then she went to Yale and graduated without loans, again thanks to Richard and Emily. As editor of the *Yale Daily News*, she also emerged with an impressive portfolio of work combined with influential contacts like her grandfather, his friends, as well as the Huntzbergers and their friends. But she is thoroughly lost and seems to have no tools at her disposal to right the ship.

Contrast that with where Lorelai was at 32. After walking away from her rich parents at 16 years old with a baby and no clear idea of where to go, Lorelai became a businesswoman. Though hardly destitute (Rory's father always contributed financially), Lorelai forged her own path—managing an inn before opening her own.

Or Lane. Married young and having twins very shortly after her marriage, Lane works hard as a mom and her husband Zack supports them in a manager job. Then in the evenings, they still play at local hotspots with the band they founded. It's not glamorous, but it's a good life.

Rory's exes Dean and Jess both came from less than stable families and not much money. Both are thriving. Where you start does not dictate where you finish.

and finally...

Money will blind you

Name one good thing about Logan Huntzberger. Specifically, one good quality he would still possess even if he were middle or lower class. Or even just generally wealthy. You can't do it, can you? Nope. Take away all those elaborate gifts and the stunts he and his stupid-rich friends pulled, take away his smug assurance that the world exists solely for him, and what do you have? An asshole working at Daddy's company who cheats on his fiancé with his ex-girlfriend and manipulates people under the guise of being magnanimous.

Seriously, Team Logan, what do you like about him that doesn't involve money? What does Rory like about him? That he calls her Ace and swoops in when she's in trouble? That he treats his side-piece nicely? Lorelai knew perfectly well how money can trap you in a golden cage and she tunneled her way out. One can only hope Rory will make that same discovery and be the one who will make her a priority in his life.

That's right, I'm Team Jess all the way.

Any fan of the original *Gilmore Girls* will enjoy watching the new miniseries, there is just no way to not enjoy it. I have every confidence that everyone will take away their own lessons from the show, but these were mine.

CHAPTER 26
AVERAGE ISN'T AN INSULT

I AM tired of romance novel tropes. There, I said it. I'm sick of the adults who think and act like children, the silly misunderstandings, and the weird, unnecessary drama.

Most of all, I am sick of all the **hotness**.

Yes, you heard me. I am annoyed at the ubiquity of full-blown hot people becoming the norm in fiction, especially in books.

This isn't a complaint against beauty. It's annoyance at rarity being pushed as common and the deleterious effect it's having on our idea of romance as a whole.

She has no idea she's beautiful

He needs a girl who can look past his rough exterior

Before I get too deep into my rant, if you are of the Andrew Tate/MedGold mindset that anyone scoring less than a 9 on the hotness scale should walk into the sea, I hear and respect your preferences.

But this chapter is not for you.

Shoo.

DO UGGOS DESERVE LOVE?

In the 2004 movie, _Vera Drake_, there's a subplot involving the titular character subtly arranging a marriage for her plain and painfully shy daughter with an equally plain and even more shy man from the neighborhood. It is impossibly sweet watching these two probable autists interact and rewatching the film made me realize that people who look like this have basically ceased to exist in all fiction.

Wouldn't last a day on Tinder

Is it online dating that banished average and below-average looking love stories?

Is it social media?

I'm not sure, but it all feels recent and sudden. Even

though it's not. *Vera Drake* came out in 2004 and the last time certified "Mid" Renee Zellwegger was an A-lister was, what... 2005?

As a visual medium, movies are expected to have above-average-looking people representing normies. But these attractive actors still had their own look to them. They were allowed big noses or not quite straight teeth.

It just made them more attractive, not less.

A listing of Renee Zelweegger's imperfections were actually a part of a movie script once, to great comedic effect:

You're a very special girl, Irene. Look at you.

You're just so down to earth. I mean, look at your hair. It's like you don't give a damn, you know?

And your skin's so natural. You just let it hang out, blemishes and all. You're not afraid of your flaws.

You have squinty eyes, and your face is all pursed up like you just sucked on a lemon, but you pull it off. (weak chuckle) - Jim Carrey to Renee Zellwegger *(Me, Myself and Irene)*

I saw *Me, Myself, and Irene* in the theater, and that got a big laugh. It wasn't at Renee's expense though. It was at Jim Carey's gormless delivery; he really thought he was giving her a compliment.

It seems real-life Renee got the same message we all did starting in the 2010s: Actually, being just attractive isn't enough. You have to be hot. Or die alone.

An improvement?

AVERAGE JOES WILL MAKE YOUR TOES CURL

Lest you think it's only the girls who have been held to this impossible standard, the men are getting it too in ways heretofore unseen in any medium.

Women's attraction to men has always been multi-factorial, meaning it's not just their looks that gets us besotted with them. It's a whole collection of attributes that can sometimes be difficult to verbalize.

Why then, are there now only two categories of accept-able male hotness: The 6'5, 6-pack dude-bro with a nine-incher OR rail-thin, square-jawed twink? Also with a nine-incher.

(Please stop putting Timothée Chalamet in every movie. Please and thank you.)

It's all so unnecessary, as made evident by the fact that THE BEST, most sensual kiss ever captured on film was between an average looking guy and an average looking girl.

It was Renee Zellwegger, in fact. And her kissing partner was none other than the not-at-all handsome Vincent D'Onofrio.

In the <u>Whole Wide World</u>, Renee was playing a mousy, plain school teacher, a role she did well in with her appearance. And Vinny played real-life pulp author Robert E. Howard, a sweet but weird guy. The movie came out in 1996 and it's STILL heralded as the pinnacle of romantic hotness (among women).

The proof is in the pudding, as they say. So why are writers and film makers wildly inflating the expectations of what the bar is for an acceptable boyfriend?

It's important to be fuckable the have a starring role in a romance, but what that means is different to different people, which such be reflected in different works of fiction.

Think of David Petrakus in *Speak* (both <u>book </u>and <u>movie</u>). This was a teen drama, so the rules are different, but David was an average-looking, lovable dork. He was sweet, cute. But also brave. And we were all screaming for Melinda to take down her walls and let David in.

Think of Adam Driver. Full stop. Adam Driver is. NOT. Handsome. But it doesn't matter. He has a charisma and magnetism that shines through the screen, hence all the <u>Reylo </u>nonsense. I don't think I'm being controversial by saying, "More of this please."

There are a lot of people out there in the dating market who are also charisma-filled sex pots… it just doesn't come through in the pictures. It's not until you shake their hand, look them in the eye, get a whiff of their perfume/cologne that you sit up and take notice.

I won't tell authors what they should do in their fiction; I wouldn't dream of messing with your money.

I'll only say that as a consumer, I would like a wider variety of fictional people to be attracted to, and I think the swaths of terminally-online single people would benefit from it.

PART EIGHT
MORALITY AND AMERICANA

CHAPTER 27

AMERICAN VULGARIAN

CAPTAIN AMERICA: *Brave New World* came out this week to tepid fanfare. A far cry from the heyday of *Captain America: The Winter Soldier*, this most recent release was marred by Marvel fatigue and by its main star, Anthony Mackie.

In front of an audience of European journalists, Mackie commented on what Captain America represents, saying, "For me, Captain America represents a lot of different things, **and I don't think the term, you know, 'America' should be one of those representations**." He added, "Like, it's about a man who keeps his word, who has honor and dignity and integrity, someone who is trustworthy and dependable."

It's no surprise Mackie said this, particularly given that his audience was foreigners. It's not in line with his politics to affirm that there's anything unique or special about Americans, their character, their qualities, or their way of life.

The only problem with that stance is that it's nonsense.

We are different. And in my humble Yankee opinion, better.

And yes, before you ask, I have traveled to and lived in other countries. Turkey, England, Germany, Belgium, and Okinawa to be specific. (Guam too, but that's a US territory).

I still think we're better. You don't have to agree, but you MUST agree that we're different from other countries, including our fellow English-speaking ones.

A recent client of mine, an Irishman by birth, is decamping from the US after the election. "I thought I found a home here, that these were my true people. I see now they're not." He lives in San Francisco, so you can guess his politics. But even being surrounded by like-minded folks in his immediate area, it seems he can no longer ignore that he's a foreigner here.

And welcome though he is, he doesn't belong.

LANGUAGE IS NOT CULTURE

The US, UK, Ireland, Australia, New Zealand, and Canada. We all speak English, but we're not the same. Likewise, Americans don't magically develop a joint culture with foreigners who speak English fluently as a second language.

The words are intelligible, but the culture remains worlds apart.

Americans, at least on the surface, value honesty and forthrightness. We don't speak in subtext, as it is often lumped in with guile and subterfuge. Most other cultures have the opposite idea, both east and west.

There's a scene in the 1993 movie, <u>Rising Sun</u>, where Sean Connery has to explain to Wesley Snipes why a

Japanese man is lying to their face. He even laughs about it. "Ah, here comes the ol' 'Sumi Masan' routine."

The corporate underling bows and apologizes profusely for a mistake he supposedly made. Except everyone in the room knows he didn't do it. Every word out of the man's mouth is a lie. He is lying so his superior will save face. This is honorable in Japanese culture.

It is not for Americans.

It's not honorable for the subordinate, who is being compelled to grovel for forgiveness for something he didn't do. He may be unjustly punished for it too.

Nor is it honorable to the person being lied to, who is tacitly being asked to feign stupidity.

And it is obscenely dishonorable for the superior, who is using his position to throw an employee under the bus. Repulsive behavior. For Americans.

But not for the Japanese, Arabs, Indians, et cetera ad infinitum.

THE ORDER OF THINGS

The slavish adherence to hierarchy, to people in positions of authority, is the primary demarcation between Americans and all others.

In watching the people of the rest of the anglosphere, I am left with the terrible conclusion that the majority of people *want* to be slaves. "Tell me what to do and make me feel safe. I'll be a good boy."

I can, I suppose, forgive other cultures for this.

Very often their hierarchy was dictated by royalty or some other God-ordained supremacy. Even if they are now democracies, that conditioning doesn't shake off easy.

Questioning authority, in their mind, is a dangerous destabilizing act. A threat.

It's the only explanation I can come up with for the anger the average citizen of Canada displays if one of their countrymen suggests that the native-born population perhaps ought not be entirely replaced by street-shitting, rapist third-worlders.

Or the anger of Britons that some of their ilk had the cheek to vote to leave the European Union.

Or the rage of Australians that some of their brethren dared step outside their front door when the government decreed they mustn't leave their homes. For years.

We have some of this in America too, of course. It drives much of the culture war. But even left-leaning Americans are still Americans.

A Russian will openly laugh at you for getting shaken down by a government official or scammed in any way. You're a chump and you deserved it, they say.

We don't say that.

We say if the government or its agents aren't doing what they are supposed to, then by golly, we will make them. We're not doing this passive aggressive, malicious compliance nonsense.

We're not Europeans.

Anthony Mackie is right that people of any nationality *can* be someone who "keeps his word, who has honor and dignity and integrity, someone who is trustworthy and dependable."

But really, how dependable can you be if you fold like a cheap suit anytime someone in a uniform tells you to stop exercising your rights? Or worse, informs you that you don't actually have those rights anymore. Because he, the uniformed person, decides what rights you do and don't have.

Truth, Justice, and the American Way means backing up honor and dignity and integrity with a hard word when it's needed, even to police, military, and elected officials.

They are not "our betters," no matter how fervently they think they are.

And we are happy to remind them of that.

Americans understand that every unjust order, every governmental overstep, is a game of "would you rather…"

- Would you rather do as you're told or lose your job?
- Would you rather tolerate an act of disrespect or lose the only person willing to sit with you at lunch?
- Would you rather stop your personal crusade… or be killed?

When you tell someone (or a group) NO, you are making a choice. You are making a stand.

How much are you willing to sacrifice for freedom, for your personal principles? And what are you willing to tolerate for comfort and security?

The answer is not simple. Ever. But it's something Americans as a whole seem much more willing to grapple with than other cultures.

We don't do the "tall poppy" syndrome here. We don't do "mind your betters."

We are a loud, disagreeable, and vulgar people.

And that's just fine with me.

CHAPTER 28
SORRY, BOOMERS. FIELD OF DREAMS DOESN'T WORK

FIELD OF DREAMS has an emotional stranglehold on men of a certain age.

I understand why. It embodies and encourages the better part of our nature and that of America in general. Plus, baseball, for reasons that escape me, is our national pastime.

I regret to inform you, it is not an outstanding movie.

It qualifies as good. But one massive flaw kept me from sharing in the shiny-eyed love for the film that afflicts my father (and millions of others).

I saw it for the first time only a few years ago and was left wondering how this was ever a film.

YOU SIT ON A THRONE OF LIES

Field of Dreams hit me wrong in a way that, say, *Angels in the Outfield*, didn't. Because it's built on a lie.

If you somehow have not seen *Field of Dreams*, Kevin Costner is a man who's from a city. His father was a minor league baseball player, very distant from him, and died probably younger than he should have. They were estranged.

Kevin Costner (I don't care about the character's name and neither do you) moved to Iowa with his lovely and supportive wife. They have a corn farm and they seem to be doing okay. They're happy.

Kevin Costner is standing in the corn one day and he hears a whispered voice, *If you build it, he will come.*

This is a mentally well, mentally fit, happy, well-adjusted man who is hearing voices in the corn. When he tells his wife about it, she's perplexed, of course. Everyone would be. Neither of them panic though. They have more of a spirit of exploration about the voice.

In obedience to the voice, Kevin decides to bulldoze his corn, which is the livelihood for his family, and build a baseball diamond. The wife, again, is supportive and says basically some semblance of, "we'll make it work."

This is okay too, kind of unrealistic, but she's a hippie chick. They both "majored in the 60s" when they went to Berkeley, so some comfort with mystic concepts is to be expected. Their open-mindedness has been established. All right, fine.

The problem comes once the field is built. Once the baseball diamond is erected, these mentally stable people, with no health problems or carbon monoxide leaks in their house, look out the window and see a dead man standing in their new baseball diamond.

Shoeless Joe Jackson, played by the delicious Ray Liotta in the flower of his youth.

They know who this man is. He's not just a stranger. They know it's Shoeless Joe Jackson, who has been dead for decades. What is the response of this loving and patient wife to seeing a dead man in her yard? She pats her husband on the shoulder and says, "I'll put on some coffee."

Oh, are you? Is that what you're going to do, ma'am? You're going to put on some coffee for the long-dead baseball player in your corn?

No, I'm sorry, I'm not going to do this with you. And let me tell you why.

A RELIGION-SHAPED PLOT HOLE

I cannot speculate as to what the original draft of the script involved.

But Kevin Costner's mission in this movie had all the hallmarks of a divine instruction.

If you are of an Abrahamic faith, we believe that God, on occasion, speaks to people and tells them to do things. I would imagine that other faiths also have this, but have no familiarity with eastern traditions.

So if Kevin Costner and his wife had been depicted as devout Christians who believed in divine intervention, and if they had perhaps speculated to one another that this voice was from heaven, it would explain their behavior from soup to nuts. No incongruity to be found.

That would have been rational in terms of the story, but that's not what happened. No mention of faith is made in this movie at all. However, since they were so into the 60s, it's reasonable to assume they were not religious at all. If they were, it was in name only.

So why did they both immediately obey a voice that speaking from the corn? There's no narrative explanation for this behavior.

None.

It would even have been acceptable if they mentioned a

ghost story. "Well, the realtor told us there's long been rumors that people hear voices in the corn telling them to do things," or something like that.

There has to be some reason why hearing a voice in the corn makes you build a baseball diamond instead of taking your ass to the hospital to get an MRI. It's not reasonable.

And I know what you're thinking. *Well, Kristin, if it's fantasy, or if a matter of faith, then it's NOT reasonable. Your logic needs to take a back seat if you believe.*

I agree with you. But from the way the story was told, Kevin Costner did NOT believe in anything. He certainly didn't believe in voices with unseen owners giving him instructions, and neither did his wife.

So *Field of Dreams*, in my opinion, was not a bad movie. I very much enjoyed the emotional payoff at the end. That famous line, "Hey Dad, do you want to have a catch?"

We're a nation full of people who grew up missing their fathers growing up, or even those that didn't, miss them now that they're gone. That payoff was wonderful, the acting was wonderful, the scenery was wonderful, and James Earl Jones is wonderful in everything that he does.

And even that self-indulgent monologue he did, which seems ridiculous when the movie's over, works in the moment. You have that verisimilitude, you're in it. It's fine.

But that first leap, that first demand that we suspend our disbelief when Shoeless Joe Jackson is standing in that baseball diamond, for me, falls flat. It wasn't earned.

If I had been given the novelized version to edit, I would have had some notes for the client who submitted it.

CHAPTER 29
THE MORALITY OF
TAKING VOWS

GROWING *up is recognizing your own selfishness and/or cowardice.*

Social media and global connection have one thing clear—a lot of people join service professions to facilitate their own needs rather than to actually serve.

This is why becoming a priest or a nun has a years-long discernment process—to weed out the people who don't belong there.

People like me.

Like all high schoolers, I waffled on what to do with my life. It was the late 90s, so college was the default. Anything else was frowned upon. But I didn't want to. I was sick of school.

That left two equally appealing options: Join the military, just like every generation of my family since we stepped off the boat

Or...

Join the convent.

That was an option that surprised everyone around

me. I toyed with the goth look, swore like a sailor, and loved tattoos, motorcycles, and hard rock music.

But I loved the church too. I loved going to Mass and the clarity of purpose I always felt after receiving the Eucharist.

I also loved the idea of living in an all-female community, never being expected to date or marry, and never having to worry about grown-up things like bills or mortgages.

Also, I would be lying if I didn't tell you the movie *Sister Act* didn't have a little bit of influence in the appeal.

Like Sister Mary Clarence (Whoopie Goldberg), I wanted to use my skills and passions to help struggling communities. Specifically, I wanted to teach.

WHAT KIND OF NUN TO BE?

The cloister was never an option. Not for me. I don't knock the power of prayer, but I always struggled to maintain focus during the rosary and have NEVER slipped into the kind of contemplative trance many cloistered nuns experience.

It's too loud in my head.

But teaching was something I wanted to do and both the convents I looked at had teaching ministries.

A full habit was also important. I don't agree with clergy and religious wearing street clothes while performing their duties. The clothes you wear define how you are treated and communicate who you are. Complain about it all you like, but actually, you can judge a book by its cover. And you should.

My first choice was Mount St. Michael's Marian Order

in Spokane Washington. They were perfect, honestly. Except...

They are not in communion with the Vatican. After the Second Vatican Council, some orders formed the Traditional Catholic Faith, which rejects Vatican II. Mount St. Michael's and their order of nuns were among them. That didn't work for me.

Instead, I settled on the Dominican Sisters of St. Cecilia, which were exactly the types of sisters I wanted to join. Their vocations director was responsive, personable, and emailed me daily, answering every stupid little question I had.

Embarrassingly I do not remember her name. But I do remember that she was an Army veteran. She chose to serve her country first. And when she was done, the convent still called to her.

ANSWERING HARD QUESTIONS

"Why do you feel called to be a nun?"

I didn't struggle to answer her first question, but I felt my resolve wavering over the course of our long correspondence and the points she raised to help me with deciding on my future.

The Sister was the one who pointed out:

- I was still a teenager and wouldn't even be old enough to vote when I graduated high school.
- I had never traveled alone.
- I came from a good home with attentive parents, so I never had the option to choose to sin, at least in a big way.

My morality had largely been formed by the fear of getting caught. Not by seeking goodness. In other words, a child's morality.

Though I didn't listen to my parents' advice at that time, I did listen to Sister. She had gone through the same struggle as me, and she wanted me to make the right choice.

When I joined the Marines right out of high school, I hadn't given up the idea of being a nun entirely.

I'll be back, I told myself.

But I wouldn't be. Because the pull I felt to the convent was never truly about serving God; it was always about serving myself. And there were far more comfortable avenues for that.

The military obviously didn't work out for me as a career. But it DID work out in that it clarified my mission in life. And it wasn't to be a nun. It was to grow into a proper adult, one worth knowing, and then to be a wife.

As it turns out, those hideously-behaved teenage boys grow up to be rather dashing men, and one in particular was the right husband for me.

I still wonder where the other path would have led me. If I could have been Sister Thomas More, like I intended— remembered as someone's favorite teacher. Maybe it would have worked out.

But I think my life unfolded, as things always do, exactly as God intended.

PART NINE
REPENTANCE AND SPIRITUAL RECKONING

CHAPTER 30
YOUR WORDS MEAN NOTHING

STOP me if you've heard this one before. A young man suspects his wife of cheating and confronts her with his suspicions. The wife, cornered, admits to it, explaining through tears why she felt driven to such misbehavior.

The husband, a Christian who loves his wife, offers to work through this together. The wife is grateful and says she is sorry for hurting him.

But...

Her behavior doesn't change. She doesn't want to give her husband access to her phone or social media accounts, even though those were the venues of her affair.

"I said I was sorry. I didn't even *have* to come clean. You should trust me." When the husband says that trust is earned, the wife brings out the trump card:

"It's not very Christian of you not to forgive me when I asked for it."

This is a heavily simplified conversation, but it happens every day in a variety of contexts. Party A egregiously wrongs Party B. Party A says sorry. Party B is allowed no further discussion of the wrongdoing. After all, "God knows my heart."

There is much discourse these days about the life-coachification of the Christian church, with most of the criticism going toward evangelical congregations. They focus on feelings, fellowship (consensus), and inclusion, rather than enforcing the standards set forth by Jesus and, later, Peter.

Everybody wants to talk about forgiveness and redemption. But they skip over contrition and repentance. Those feel icky to talk about. "Stop shaming me!" the mega-church attendees insist. "You're ruining the vibe, man."

Christian movies like to feature forgiveness and repentance as major themes but… those movies don't quite resonate. Even with believers. The cringe is too strong.

Surprise of all surprises, Hollywood actually did it justice. In 2010, _Devil_ was hardly a box-office smash, but it was one of the better religious horror movies of the time, largely because it showed us an aspect of Christianity that often gets glossed over these days.

Yes, you can be forgiven no matter how badly you have sinned, but there is a price of admission. One that goes way beyond saying you're sorry.

A GALLERY OF ROGUES

In a high-rise office building, five people get into an elevator. Three men and two women. Only one gets out—even though his sins were arguably the worst.

First, there's **Vince**.

Obviously, he's a smarmy asshole. We know he's a

creep just by looking at him. He behaves like a creep from the get-go and though we don't learn until later he started a ponzi scheme, we know immediately he's scum.

Then, there is "**the old woman**."

She is never named, but is introduced as your classic Karen. Nagging, unpleasant, expecting others to cater to her while being a burden to those around her. We find out later through the police characters that this woman makes a habit of snatching things from other women's purses when they're not looking.

Ben is a security guard, a temp actually.

This is his first day working in the building. The temp agency who hired him obviously didn't bother with a background check, because Ben has a record of assault. He's a violent guy, one who is familiar with the stages of rigor mortis, so maybe there are more crimes he wasn't caught for.

Sarah is young, entitled, and pretty.

Vince, being a ponzi guy, immediately clocks her as being filthy rich. Quiet luxury rich. How did she come by all that money? Years of blackmailing rich men, only to land a whale of a husband—the heir to a billion-dollar empire. We can assume there was no prenup, because she is in that elevator on the way to see a divorce attorney, one who specializes in forensic accounting.

Tony is a working class guy who doesn't fit in with the rest of the group.

A former Marine and Afghanistan war vet, Tony is best prepared to tackle the strange situation unfolding in the elevator. He also feels he has something to prove. Five years ago, he drove drunk and killed a woman and her child. Calling no one, Tony scribbled out "I'm sorry" on the back of a car wash coupon and left it on the mangled car he crashed into. And then left the scene.

And watching all of them like some kind of guardian angel is **Detective Bowden**.

Called to the scene to investigate a jumper suicide in that building, Bowden is there to observe through cameras the horror that seems to have no explanation. Newly sober, Bowden struggles with rage. You see, his wife and child were killed by a drunk driver five years ago.

Ramirez: [The Devil] never does this in secret. There's a reason we're the audience.

THE DEVIL GETS HIS DUE

Of all the people in the elevator, Vince is the only one who can't pull off the act of being a decent human being. He doesn't have the physiognomy for it. So it makes sense he is the first to die. After the elevator jolts to a stop and any attempt to get it moving again fails, the lights start to flicker and the occupants get real antsy.

Finally, the flights flicker off. In the pitch black, the mirror glued to the wall is smashed, and when the lights come back up, a piece of glass has been shoved into Vince's neck. He bleeds out in record time. Now there are four people left, and no one knows which is the killer.

The old woman is the second to die. The lights turn off again, and when they come back on, our elderly harridan is hanging from the rafters. Now there are three people left.

With the old woman being strung up like that, it excludes Sarah as the guilty party. She doesn't have the strength.

That leaves Ben and Tony to stare each other down, Ben positioning himself as Sarah's protector—something she orchestrated from the start. Shortly after the elevator stopped, Sarah accused Vince of groping her, clinging to Ben and begging him "Don't let him touch me."

After Vince is killed, Tony uses his mechanics skills to take off a light panel with the intention of climbing up to the next access panel in the shaft.

What does Sarah do? She screams: "He's escaping! He wants to get away with it!"

This drives Ben to grab hold of Tony and drag him back in the elevator, threatening to kill him if he tries to leave.

No one even suspected Tony of being the one to stab Vince. Why would they? Was Sarah trying to stop him from getting help? Or maybe she just couldn't help herself. This is her pattern.

Tony sees her for what she is.

Don't you see what she's doing? Chick's a twist... that's what we used to call people like her in the Marines.

Suddenly out of the blue, everybody would start fighting with each other. Tempers would flare, people would start getting hurt.

But then we realized it's just the new guy telling everybody what other people said, stirring shit up where there wasn't any.

Until one night when we beat the living shit out of that twist.

And then, just like that, everything would go back to normal.

By now, Detective Bowden has ordered all three of them to keep their hands on the wall, facing away from each other in a futile attempt to keep control until the fire department can cut through concrete to get to them.

But the lights go out again, and when they come up, Ben is on the floor, his neck twisted all the way around.

Tony and Sarah have a Mexican standoff, each holding out a piece of broken mirror at the other, terrified.

Tony has to know that Sarah is not strong enough to have twisted a human head around like that. But by this point, everyone knows they're dealing with something more than human.

LOOKING YOUR SIN IN THE FACE

Bowden: According to your story, how would I save them?

Ramirez: There's no easy answer. You're never gonna get these people to see themselves as they really are. 'cause it's the lies that we tell ourselves, they introduce us to him.

Tony knows Sarah is a bad person. He doesn't know about the blackmail or the impending divorce rape of the hapless rich husband. He only knows that Sarah is nasty and likes to cause chaos wherever she goes.

Even still, when the lights go out again, and they come on to reveal Sarah's throat has been cut, he rushes immediately to help.

But it's too late. For her, and for him.

The old woman, the corpse with the broken neck, stands up, revealing herself as the devil.

Tony looks up at her in horror, but doesn't recoil. He knows what she's there for. Instead of begging for his life, he begs for Sarah's. "Take me instead. I deserve this."

This offer disgusts the devil, rather than moves him.

"You think you're good? You think you should be forgiven?"

No, he doesn't.

And he doesn't plead for Sarah because he thinks she deserves it either. She doesn't. Sarah isn't sorry for anything. But he knows between the two of them, he deserves damnation more. A debt must be paid, and he is willing to pay it.

But it's not Tony's contrition, his sorrow, or even his willingness to die for Sarah, that moves the devil, that takes away his power to drag Tony to hell.

It's when Tony grabs the police radio and broadcasts to everyone in the building, including police: "I killed a mother and her son on Bethlehem Pike five years ago. Uh... It was a hit-and-run and I was never caught. I'm so sorry."

And he is. He is sorry. He will atone. He will make recompense. He will go forth and sin no more.

That is what denies the devil his claim on a soul.

"Damn. I really wanted you."

The lights come back on, and everything starts working again. The elevator smoothly makes its way to the ground floor, where the fire crew is there to meet it. The doors open to reveal Tony alive, sitting in the elevator with three bloody corpses. But the old woman is gone.

REPENTANCE IS THE PRICE OF SALVATION

What would you do if you found out you'd just spent the whole day trying to save the life of the man who killed your family? The man who took everything from you? Who drove you to drink and, one dark night, hold a gun to your head?

Bowden is there to arrest Tony for the crime he has just confessed to, and tells his partner he will take him to the station. In the car, we see him battling the rage.

After driving silently, Bowden tells Tony who he is.

"That was my family on Bethlehem Pike. That was my son. I've been waiting for this moment for five years. All the things I'd say to you and what I'd do."

Tony listens, the same mournful acceptance on his face as in the elevator.

"The thing is, I forgive you."

And we believe him. Because there is no lip service being paid in that car, no virtue signaling for cameras. No transactional "grace" being given for the sake of one's own ego.

There is only a man grievously wronged witnessing the real, tactile repentance of the one who wronged him. And feeling the weight of rage being lifted from his shoulders.

Catholics recite the Act of Contrition when we go to confession. Contrition being the affliction of the soul or a heartfelt sadness at our own wrongdoing.

But that's not enough.

Repentance is one step further. It's changing course, changing your mindset, changing your soul to never even be capable of such evil again.

The feelings without the action are meaningless.

People love to ask, "Are Christians REQUIRED to forgive people?" You're asking the wrong question.

The real question is, in the face of true repentance, is any Christian capable of *not* forgiving? Probably not.

Because we all know what it looks like. We feel it down to our bones when we witness the resolution of a sinner to be different, to be better, and do whatever is needed to atone for what they've done.

And those who think their own guilty conscience is enough, who think they can skip out on the atonement part of the equation... you're not fooling anyone with your self-help, new-age platitudes.

Least of all God.

ABOUT KRISTIN MCTIERNAN

Stories are how humans learn and grow, so telling them correctly is a skill that could very well change someone's life.

With over 15 years of experience as a full-time ghost-writer and editor, I've been helping people turn words into art, something that has become much harder in the age of rapid-release "content."

I am dedicated to meaningful storytelling—why it's important and how it informs our culture. If you want to follow me on that exploration, you can find me:

- On Fictional Influence, my Substack publication, where I have new articles every week on writing, movies, morality, and the unending gender war
- On YouTube as The Nonsense-Free Editor
- And for writers, you can hire me as an editor, ghostwriter, or indie publication consultant at The Nonsense-Free Editor

- If you're a masochist who doesn't mind profanity, you can follow me on Twitter and Substack.

I also write fiction, which should come as no surprise to you. And you can find all my novels at Kristinmctiernan.com.

Thank you for reading! If you want to stay up to date on new releases, including volume 2 of the Fictional Influence collection, then be sure to subscribe to Fictional Influence.

https://www.fictionalinfluence.com

www.ingramcontent.com/pod-product-compliance
Lightning Source LLC
Chambersburg PA
CBHW071738270326
41928CB00013B/2722